family
inc.

JEREMY P. TARCHER / PENGUIN

a member of Penguin Group (USA) Inc.

New York

family inc.

Office-Inspired Solutions to
Reduce the Chaos in Your Home
(and Save Your Sanity!)

CAITLIN
AND
ANDREW FRIEDMAN

JEREMY P. TARCHER/PENGUIN
Published by the Penguin Group
Penguin Group (USA) Inc., 375 Hudson Street, New York, New York 10014, USA •
Penguin Group (Canada), 90 Eglinton Avenue East, Suite 700, Toronto, Ontario
M4P 2Y3, Canada (a division of Pearson Penguin Canada Inc.) • Penguin Books
Ltd, 80 Strand, London WC2R 0RL, England • Penguin Ireland, 25 St Stephen's
Green, Dublin 2, Ireland (a division of Penguin Books Ltd) • Penguin Group
(Australia), 707 Collins Street, Melbourne, Victoria 3008, Australia
(a division of Pearson Australia Group Pty Ltd) • Penguin Books India Pvt Ltd,
11 Community Centre, Panchsheel Park, New Delhi–110 017, India • Penguin
Group (NZ), 67 Apollo Drive, Rosedale, Auckland 0632, New Zealand
(a division of Pearson New Zealand Ltd) • Penguin Books, Rosebank
Office Park, 181 Jan Smuts Avenue, Parktown North 2193,
South Africa • Penguin China, B7 Jaiming Center, 27 East Third
Ring Road North, Chaoyang District, Beijing 100020, China

Penguin Books Ltd, Registered Offices:
80 Strand, London WC2R 0RL, England

Most Tarcher/Penguin books are available at special quantity discounts for
bulk purchase for sales promotions, premiums, fund-raising, and educational
needs. Special books or book excerpts also can be created to fit specific needs.
For details, write Penguin Group (USA) Inc. Special Markets,
375 Hudson Street, New York, NY 10014.

ISBN 978-1-58542-942-4

Printed in the United States of America
1   3   5   7   9   10   8   6   4   2

BOOK DESIGN BY ELLEN CIPRIANO

While the authors have made every effort to provide accurate telephone
numbers, Internet addresses, and other contact information at the time of
publication, neither the publisher nor the authors assume any responsibility for
errors, or for changes that occur after publication. Further, the publisher does not
have any control over and does not assume any responsibility
for author or third-party websites or their content.

Some of the names and identifying characteristics of individuals mentioned in this
book have been changed to protect the privacy of those involved.

To our children, Declan and Taylor,
who brought love, happiness, and
a little chaos into our lives

contents

family
inc.

preface

What if we told you that investing just one hour per week could lead to a better marriage and a happier home?

What if we told you that, while it's good to leave the office at the front door, treating your household a bit more like an office could actually be the first step toward mastering the chaos that has overtaken your life?

What if we told you that many of the problems you're having as a couple are probably nothing more than by-products of poor time management and stress?

What if we told you that it's possible to evenly divide household chores, errands, and responsibilities without fighting over who does what?

Well, these are all things that we've discovered over ten years of marriage. During that time, like all but the luckiest few, we've had our ups and downs. Ironically, it was at our lowest point as a couple that we discovered the road back to happiness by drawing on our working lives—of all things—for guidance.

This book shares how we did it, and how any family can benefit from the lessons we learned along the way.

The Moment of Inspiration That Led to This Book

It all started when we were seated across from each other at a conference table during a job interview and fell in love. Caitlin was looking to break into public relations, and Andrew had a job available on his team at a midsize agency. After a great conversation (which honestly felt a little bit like a blind date), we began working together. Over the course of the next year, one thing led to another, as they say, and we started dating, at first secretly, and then—when we were sure it was the real thing—publicly.

Those were the easy days. We didn't have a care in the world. We both had good jobs and our own apartments. We went out or stayed in as we pleased. It was a storybook romance that culminated in an unforgettable wedding. But too soon after the toasts were made, the cake was cut, and the caterer paid, our life together got complicated. We bought a house. We had twins. We sold a house. Andrew launched a freelance writing career. Caitlin started a public relations business and then left the field to become a freelance writer before jumping back into corporate America. We dealt with the roller-coaster financial life of freelancers, as well as the usual complement of personal dramas—adjusting to parenthood, navigating illness and other crises—all the while trying to find a little time to spend with each other. As the pressures of life and work piled up, we found ourselves having the kinds of arguments we swore we never would—bickering over money, time, sex, peace, independence, and sleep . . . or lack thereof.

Sound familiar?

When did this happen? When had we morphed into the kinds of people who struggle to make time for everything from an hour at the gym to an after-work drink with friends? This wasn't what we signed up for!

Like many contemporary working couples, we found ourselves at sea, so focused on basic survival—simply striving to get through the week without dropping too many balls—that we fell out of touch with everything, from small tasks, like cleaning the house, to the larger, more important concerns that give our lives meaning, like enjoying our kids and each other, or planning for our long-term dreams, such as owning our own home.

There isn't a faster track to arguing than when two depleted working parents find themselves faced with school clothes that suddenly don't fit ("Are *all* of his jeans this short?"), having to scurry to the store for the tenth time in a week for basic household items and food (running out of baby formula was a personal specialty of ours), or opening an overdue—and therefore credit-damaging—electric bill found buried in the neglected mountain of mail by the front door. All of those little things build up to a constant, marriage-threatening drumbeat of tension, stress, and conflict, and all too often, the overall effect sneaks up on a couple. When you are already overwhelmed with trying to excel as a parent, a professional, *and* a partner, recognizing that there's a problem—let alone creating the time and mental space to solve it—can seem beyond daunting.

But after argument #345 about something as ridiculous as who was going to pick up the gift for a child's birthday party we were going to *that very afternoon*, we realized that something had to change. For the sake of our sanity and the health of our marriage, we had to take back control of our schedule, time, and responsibilities. We skipped couples therapy and self-help books because, frankly, even at our darkest point—when our increasingly fraying tempers led us to quarrel several times a day—we recognized that our problems weren't emotional but *practical*.

We finally saw the light one snowy winter weekend on a long drive home from an out-of-town trip. With the kids napping in the backseat, we began talking about all the things we had to deal with, get done, and even just think about. Before we knew it, we were having a joint panic attack. There were so many things that needed to be addressed that by the time we'd listed the last five, we couldn't remember the first.

"You know what we need?" Caitlin asked, then answered her own question with the two words that changed our lives: "A meeting."

Andrew knew right away what she meant. When we used to work together in an office, we had a lot to juggle: employees, clients, budgets, and even our romantic relationship. But it never felt overwhelming. A big reason was the weekly sit-down our professional team held. No matter how busy we were, every Monday we gathered around a table with our colleagues and reviewed the week's to-do list, deciding who would handle what and by when. At the end of that meeting, all the sundry tasks required to keep things on track had been divvied up into manageable lists for each member of the team.

Inspired by that memory, Caitlin fished a notebook and pen out of her purse. While Andrew drove, we began assembling our own personal list the way we used to create a professional one. Within a few minutes of free-associating, we had an inventory of what needed to happen. Then we began deciding who would do what and by when. By the time we parked the car at home, Caitlin ripped two sheets of paper from her notebook—his and hers to-do lists for the week.

The exercise took less than an hour, but the next week went so well—each of us crossing things off our respective lists according to when we had the time and energy to deal with them—that the following Saturday as we were having our morning coffee, we both had the same inspiration: "We need another meeting."

Before we knew it, we were having meetings *every* Saturday. The results were so life-altering that a broader thought occurred to us: Why not take it a step further? Why not apply other workplace systems and skills to running our household rather than allowing it to run us?

Some of this happened organically; for example, as we divvied up tasks in that weekly meeting, we realized that we each gravitated naturally toward certain roles. In his writing life, Andrew is a cookbook specialist, so he found himself volunteering to do the food shopping and meal planning. He had also always had a gift for math, so he became the house bookkeeper, a role that didn't exist until we found ourselves on the brink of depleting our bank account for the third time in a year. Caitlin had always been fascinated by the creativity and imagination that goes into creating toys and children's books, so when it came to buying clothes, presents, and furniture for our own kids, she took the lead. She is also great at multitasking, so she took on jobs that could be interwoven with her own work, for instance, running to the bank, registering the kids for camp, and ordering groceries online during lunch breaks.

We soon realized that although we didn't use the term "job descriptions," that's what we had essentially created for ourselves, just as we used to have in our old jobs at the public relations agency. Only, in our home, we had created the descriptions and responsibilities based on strengths and interests, so it was a more natural division of labor, and, even better, tasks were getting done more quickly.

Our weekly meeting was a revelation to us. So were the "job descriptions" that organically evolved from it. Almost immediately we recognized that the more organized we were, the fewer arguments we had. It sounds like such an obvious observation, but like so many married couples, we had never seen the forest for the trees. Once we thought about it, though, it was *so* clear to us that *organization*—while it might not seem romantic—was the key to returning to that romantic place we used to occupy so effortlessly. Think about it: Successful offices and companies run smoothly because of *systems and protocols*, from job descriptions to employee manuals to regular meetings. Those things are a given in a professional workplace, and the more smoothly an office runs, the more fun it is to work there. But most people (including, for the longest time, *us*) leave their offices at night and forget the lessons we learn every day, coming home to a no less complicated place with its own issues of maintenance, finance, supplies, and cleanliness . . . and just expect it to run itself, when the truth is that a disorganized home is no more fun than a disorganized office.

Let's take it a step further. Think about the relationships you've developed in office situations. If the office is efficient and upbeat, friendships are forged in mutual success and the great times shared by the people who achieved them, and attaining goals together deepens relationships. In contrast, consider the taint that sullies the often dysfunctional relationships developed in a poisonous work environment; they're not rooted in good times, and often don't last beyond the completion of a project.

The same principles apply to a household. When things run smoothly, when there is minimal confusion, you can focus on the positive, you can achieve great things, and your relationship will be enhanced by what this allows you to accomplish, both independently and as a couple. There's also time for fun, both planned and spontaneous.

Once we had this realization, we began applying other office principles to our home: We schedule. We budget. We plan. We "manage growth." We set goals. We've even adopted some of the software and documents that make an office run efficiently: We created a checklist of grocery and household items to expedite weekly shopping, saving both time and mental energy. We posted a shared social calendar in the kitchen that eliminated the dreaded double-booking surprises. We bought a bill caddy organized by payment due date to prevent those heart-stopping moments when we used to wonder if our phone service was about to be suspended.

Applying these professional systems to the home might not sound romantic, but it took almost no time to implement them, and the almost-instant result was that our shared life became more manageable and, therefore, more relaxed and conducive to good times and romance. By compartmentalizing the relationship-killing discussions about the mundane, office-like concerns that can smother passion, we created more time and attention for ourselves and each other. All those little "I thought you took care of that" arguments melted away, as did the resentments over who was carrying more or less of the household load. And if those concerns ever did arise, we had a weekly forum—the meeting—for adjusting the plan and working them out.

Ever since those formative days when we first discovered the power of the weekly meeting, we have been committed to touching base for about an hour each Saturday to map out the week, catching each other up on the responsibilities we manage and "assigning" miscellaneous items as they arise. When we see other couples struggling, or when they share their frustrations with us over a drink or dinner, we share our little secret, and we can almost see the lightbulb go off over their heads. "Of course!" they say. "That makes perfect sense." And it does. And the cherry on top of this ritual is that there are direct emotional benefits to the meeting as well, because it becomes a repository for all the daily obligations, stresses, and concerns that otherwise might go unsaid, ricochet around in our heads, and threaten to undo us.

So here it is: a book full of ideas, stories, suggestions, lessons, advice, and experiences from many perspectives to help you change how you run your household. We ask you to go into this with an open mind, to stay honest with yourself and your family, and, most important, to be willing to try something new.

1

getting on the same page

SETTING A PERSONAL AGENDA

You have picked up this book for a reason: Your household needs a major overhaul. You know that things aren't working as smoothly as they could be and that important details are slipping through the cracks. But are you both aware of it and ready to try a new technique? Changing the way you do things at home takes a little time, a little energy, and a lot of communication, because just as with any transition in an office—new systems, protocols, managers—everyone needs to be on the same page before anything can move forward. The interviews, surveys, lists, ideas, tips, and advice offered in this first chapter will help you get synched up with your partner so you can make the most of the lessons featured throughout the rest of the book.

To start with, accept that because you have been doing things on the fly, you may have no idea what needs to get done, how much time is really spent on the household, or even what your partner contributes. This chapter will ask you to work together to create a snapshot of the way the home runs now, in order to develop a better understanding of what specifically has to change.

This chapter begins with a survey that asks you to track the things that have to be tackled on a daily, weekly, and monthly basis, taking note of how often they fall through the cracks. This list will be the foundation for what's discussed in several upcoming chapters, including ones about the weekly meeting itself, job responsibilities, and conflict resolution.

To shed light on where both of you may be coming from and what requires adjustment, we ask each of you to sit down and draft a few lists, from "I wish I didn't have to . . ." (chores you can't stand) and "I'm great at . . ." (skills you feel good about and enjoy) to "We just can't agree about . . ." (recurring issues) and "I wish we did more of . . . and less of . . ." If you are anything like us, you might be surprised by what you learn about each other during this process, including the possibility of having two very different ideas of what the issues are in the first place.

To help convince you that you're not the only ones feeling overwhelmed, we've included an interview with Lisa and Mark, a couple currently struggling with balance and communication who really need a to-do list so they can get on the same page. Their situation illustrates how setting aside a little time each week to connect about what needs to be done at home can turn conflict into collaboration. Throughout the chapter you will find links, tips, advice, and reading recommendations to help you save time, money, and your sanity. Most important, we include methods for strengthening your relationship, such as discussing favorite things to do as a couple, sharing how you would spend a free day, and brainstorming a few ideas for what to do with all of that downtime *Family Inc.* will help you carve out.

Working Families Today

While researching this book, we started talking to couples about life as a working family. We soon realized that we had a lot in common. *All* of us feel that our plates are a little too full. *All* of us feel as if we are teetering on the edge of losing ourselves in the monotony or chaos of running a home. *All* of us want more time to return to the couple we were in the "before."

Before assuming that there's a problem with your relationship, recognize that most marriages these days face enormous pressures brought on by huge social and financial changes. With women at work—now more than ever the primary breadwinners for their families—and men taking a more active parenting role, the traditional household model is obsolete. Just watch an episode of *Mad Men* and you'll realize how dramatically things have shifted on the home front since our parents' generation. Forty years ago, there was no question about who was packing the school lunch, darning a sock, or cooking the Sunday pot roast. These days, we can't make any assumptions about who is doing what because we are *all* doing too much. The upshot is that rather than adhering to outdated gender roles, every modern two-career couple has to determine a division of labor that works for them. Until they do, the lack of clarity can put a huge strain on any marriage.

This book is about pinpointing what has to get done and how it's going to get done. It's about accepting that there are no preassigned roles to fall back on. It's about *not* forgetting that you spend the bulk of your weekday cranking through your work to-do list with little conflict. It's about bringing home your efficient, talented, and focused professional self and not letting relationship baggage get in the way of getting things done.

When Things Aren't Working

Bickering with your partner isn't the only indicator that things have to change; it's just the most obvious one. If one of you is complaining every week or even every day that you are doing more than the other, then the balance at home is off. But there are also subtle signs that the system needs tweaking, such as when bills are late, appointments are missed, calls go unreturned, gifts aren't bought, long-term plans such as wills and college funds are never dealt with, a budget is never made or followed, friendships go unattended, you can't remember your last date night, you aren't living the way you want to live. While none of these are earth-shattering events, they can gradually erode the quality of your life and your future. Never mind the impact it can have on your relationship. Signs to watch out for include feeling resentful about how much you do and being overwhelmed by how much needs to be done. You know the symptoms: a house that is never quite clean, kids who live without a schedule, constant scrambling at the last minute, an often-empty refrigerator, and basic neglect of the details that help make your house a home. Whether it's a temporary situation brought about by a massive project at the office or just the way life has become, when things slip, it puts tremendous strain on your relationship. Ideally, your home is your sanctuary—the place to unwind and get support and relaxation. But honestly, nowadays we all juggle so much that our homes can feel like more work. We expect that our work life is complicated, busy, and stressful, but home should be the opposite. Neither has to be true all of the time. Work can be busy, but it can also go through periods of being quiet and even relaxing. Home can get crazy but not all of the time. To navigate the busy times, we suggest changing your expectations for how things "should" be. When things aren't working, it's just a sign that systems, priorities, and even attitudes need some readjustment.

A True Story: Is This You?

Lisa and Mark are two busy professionals with a household of three children under the age of seven. Mark is in sales, which often requires him to travel, especially during the holidays and other busy family times. Lisa works from home as a copywriter a few days a week, but the demands of her position mean that she can't stray far from her home office. They had a nanny but that wasn't quite enough, so they recently hired an au pair who now lives with them. Even with all of the help they have, the household is a beast to manage and, as you will see from the interview below, most of it falls on Lisa. This is a couple that could really benefit from stepping back and taking a hard look at who is doing what and why. We've offered some advice following Lisa's responses, and if you find some of the details in this situation familiar, know that this book will really help you.

Who Does What Around the House?

Lisa tells us that she does "twenty-five to thirty percent more of the housework" than her husband. Mark "pays bills, takes out the garbage, and occasionally will throw in a load of laundry or do the grocery shopping." But in terms of the kids' schedules, such as "the lunches, the doctor's appointments, the meals, the cleaning, the bed making, the general tidying up," Lisa does it. This isn't entirely Mark's fault, because, Lisa later admits, "Part of it is that I can't stand a messy house. And with three kids under the age of seven running around, it gives me a sense of order and control." She wonders how Mark is "blissfully unaffected by the chaos" and is astounded that it doesn't bother him at all if dishes stack up in the sink. *We* wonder if he is unaware or if he assumes she is going to take care of it when Lisa tells us, "Whenever we get ready to go on a family trip, he packs his own bag. I pack one for our six-year-old, four-year-old, and three-year-old before packing my own."

If any of this sounds familiar, then you will find the chapter on job descriptions helpful. Lisa and Mark need to create a full to-do list and review it together. He may not be aware of what goes into running the family, and seeing it on paper may help communicate that. Lisa is obviously building up resentment about the situation, but it doesn't seem as if she is sharing her frustrations or suggesting creative ways to change things. Just think about colleagues at work who aren't pulling their weight. In most cases, they are confronted and redirected. If this is happening at home—if the division of labor is blatantly imbalanced—then say something.

Who Manages the Kids?

Given Lisa's response to the above, we weren't surprised when Lisa said, "In terms of the kids, I definitely oversee their schedules." But we thought it was interesting that she "has no problem delegating the day." Lisa will ask Mark to bring the boys to a soccer game while she takes their daughter to a birthday party. Mark "loves tennis, so he will happily take the kids and teach them how to play." Lisa loves swimming, so she is teaching them to swim. But at the end of the day she says, "It's sixty percent me and forty percent him" when it comes to the kids.

Since Lisa doesn't seem to have a problem delegating, perhaps she would benefit from doing more of it. Mark's willingness to take direction is actually a good place to start. She should guide him to do more things around the house. Putting on the manager hat, we would recommend that Lisa sit down and explain what needs to be done and suggest a few tasks that Mark could take on. If there are jobs that Mark hasn't done before, then, as Lisa would with any new employee, she could spend a few minutes training him. In this case, the delegation needs to be on Lisa, because we are guessing that Mark might not even be aware of how much his wife is taking on at home. Lastly, we want to remind all readers that once a task has been delegated and you have taken the time to do the training and made yourself available for any follow-up questions, let the person do the job. Micromanaging is a waste of everyone's time.

How Is the Family Schedule Managed?

Like many of the couples we interviewed, Lisa and Mark have a big calendar where they keep track of such things as the "school schedule, after-school programs, birthday parties, and doctors' appointments." Lisa is the one who manages the schedule, telling us, "It's just faster for me to do it, because I know everyone's schedule in my head. No matter how far into the school year we are, Mark never seems to remember who should be where, when, and at what time."

If tasks can be more equally distributed, we would advise that Lisa keep her role as the overseer of the family schedule. She is clearly good at it and has a reliable memory. She is most likely only resentful of Mark's forgetfulness because their workloads are so unbalanced. If you resented a colleague at work for inadequacies in your workloads yet never spoke up, where would it get you? Not very far. This is also true at home. We would recommend that Lisa shelve any lingering resentment she has toward Mark and focus on improving the communication between them.

How Do You Two Reconnect?

Mark and Lisa have the occasional date night, but they have also discovered that while socializing with other couples is fun, "sometimes it's important to just have that one-on-one conversation to check in on where the other person is at." Additionally, like us, they have realized that spending time on "fun long-range plans ('Let's move to Hawaii when we retire!') and dreams can help keep us going when the day-to-day stuff feels overwhelming."

We couldn't agree more with this. A good balance between socializing with friends and being together as a couple is key to reconnecting, and so is spending time thinking about the big-picture fun stuff. Planning for the future together can also be a bonding exercise during times of tension. Rather than focusing too much on what is happening right now, looking ahead to where you want to be as a family one year or five years from now can help you put things in perspective.

Which Professional Skills Do You Find Most Helpful at Home?

Lisa is an excellent manager with a loyal staff at her office, so we weren't surprised when she told us that she spends "a lot of time managing our nanny and au pair." They are juggling a part-time nanny with an au pair who helps the other days and, most importantly, when Mark is on the road. As we all know, working with our children's caregivers is a complicated matter (more on this later). To do it efficiently, Lisa has mini-meetings each morning to "talk about the day, any issues that have come up, duties, projects, etc." She then follows up with them via text and e-mail. Additionally, it is Lisa's job to train the caregivers. "It's kind of like managing an assistant, except they have a much bigger job and are responsible for your children's health and happiness." Lisa makes an effort to keep the caregivers happy so they feel like "they have a partnership in the job."

As you will see later in the book, meetings are the key to keeping things on track. If you have caregivers either in or out of the house that help with your children, then you might want to consider Lisa's approach and treat them as partners.

Do You Two Have Challenges When Things Are a Little Too Much Like Business at Home?

Lisa tells us that because Mark runs his own business, she feels that he sometimes treats her "like one of his employees, questioning how I've done something." Since they are actually partners and equals, then moments when Lisa feels managed cause tension between them. She is quick to call him on it, so it isn't a pervasive issue for them. When Lisa tries to correct Mark on something he has done around the house that she feels could have been done better, he is "quick to get defensive and shut down."

Mark and Lisa have learned that it is better to treat your partner like a partner and not an employee. Even if one of you does more at this point, you are still colleagues with the same title.

Do You Have Any Tips for Enjoying Family Time?

Lisa and Mark don't get to enjoy enough family time. But they discovered that they could have a little more if, instead of watching television at the end of the day, they play board games. Lisa tells us, "It's a nice way to end the day. The kids quiet down as they concentrate on the game." On the weekends they often go hiking as a family. "Hiking gives the kids a chance to run, have fun, ask questions, and sometimes my husband and I can sneak an alone moment on the trail when they run ahead of us, and have five minutes just to talk."

Any time you can carve out five minutes of quiet time just to talk is a blessing!

No Excuses

So where do you start? To begin with, accept that you are reading this book for a reason—things aren't working at home. It most likely has nothing to do with your marriage and everything to do with how the details of your lives are being handled. We just don't have the luxury of living the way people did even twenty years ago, so we can't look to how our parents managed. Since the era of the wife doing the bulk of the housework and the child care solution being an open back door are gone, we have to find a new way to do things. For us, two people who have spent a great deal of time and energy on their professional lives, discovering that the answers to our disarray at home could be found in the office was a huge relief. We knew how to do work well; it was the home stuff that was slipping through the cracks. We'll be frank with you: This process isn't always going to be easy. We are asking you to look honestly at what you put into the household and your willingness to do more. We are also asking you to start from scratch and redefine your roles and responsibilities. On the flip side, this is an exciting opportunity to make changes that will benefit everyone. Maybe you secretly always wanted to spend more time cooking meals but felt that the kitchen wasn't yours, or maybe you assumed you didn't have the extra funds to hire a Saturday night sitter, but now you do.

One Step at a Time

To get to the point where your personal calendar is up to date, the kitchen is stocked, the birthday presents bought and wrapped, the vacation plans made, the house clean, the dentist appointment booked, the bank accounts reconciled, without doing it all yourself, you have to accept a few truths:

- Things aren't working right now.
- We are *all* busy, tired, and stressed.
- If the workload is uneven, it makes more work for one of us.
- We must make time for each other.
- We must make time for ourselves.
- We don't work for each other.
- We have a responsibility to each other to do what we say we are going to do.
- We agree not to fight about the to-do list anymore.
- We will put time into creating new systems and ways of doing things at home.
- We will not micromanage each other.
- We will communicate our own needs.

So knowing that there are no more excuses, are you ready to take the step?

What Do You Want?

Most managers have figured out that nothing motivates their employees more than having established goals for them to work toward. These could be anything from a sales target, to finishing up a major project within a set amount of time, to learning a new skill. Most of us happily work toward an objective because we want that sense of accomplishment that comes with reaching it. It feels good to finish something, to cross it off our list, and to move forward. Even more rewarding is when you are a member of a team or a company and feel that you've actively contributed to the process. To motivate yourself and your family and to keep everyone on track, we suggest that you establish a few goals. These can be short-term or long-term, big or small. Whatever you come up with, make sure that they are all achievable and will ultimately contribute to the health and happiness of your family. These might be:

- Create a free hour each weekend when everyone can do whatever they want.
- Find someone to help clean the house one day a month.

- Stop arguing about the dishes, laundry, bill paying, etc.
- Appreciate the time and energy that gets put into the house.
- Have the kids contribute more to running the house.
- Make some long-term plans together.
- Figure out a better organization system for bill paying.
- Find an accountant to help figure out finances.
- Get better at managing the people we hire to help us at home . . . including the babysitter!
- Start saving for college.
- Make a plan to buy a house.

You can write this list separately and come together to share and discuss it—maybe resetting a few priorities along the way—or you can write the list together. We use goal setting as we did at the office.

Getting to Know You

You both know things need to change, but do you agree on what isn't succeeding? Like an employee who has had a bad performance review, you might be shocked to hear what isn't working for your partner. Yes, you've been together for a while. Yes, you may know each other better than anyone. But could you list what your partner wants to do more or less of around the house? The truth is, there is always more you can learn about the other person and their point of view. More than that, we want you to see your partner differently—not as just a spouse, best friend, and co-parent, but also as a colleague with their own working style, preferences, interests, skills, and goals.

At the office, the best work comes out of a team that is truly collaborative. These are the teams that are in synch, where there is an understanding of the strengths, weaknesses, interests, and even limitations of one another. Try looking at your partner as a new coworker and colleague whom you have to get to know and accept because you are now working on an important new project together. We aren't talking about her favorite movie or whether or not she prefers red wine over white, but rather what she likes to work on, what she doesn't, how she wants the weekend to look, and what she wishes she were better at.

It will only take a few minutes to finish up these sentences, and we promise that you just might learn a thing or two about the person you're living with.

At home . . .

> I wish I didn't have to . . .
>
> My least favorite task is . . .
>
> My partner is great at . . .
>
> I am terrible at . . .

I need to learn how to . . .

We just can't agree on how to . . .

It would be worth it for me to hire someone to . . .

I wish it was my job to . . .

If . . .

I had an extra hour each night, I would . . .

On the weekend . . .

I would like to spend less time . . .

I would like to spend more time . . .

I wish we didn't . . .

Review Yourself

What do annual reviews have to do with what kind of partner you are at home? A lot, because how you are as an employee—the good, bad, and ugly—offers you clues about how you are and how you could be as a partner at home. Your ability to balance the department budget, find the ideal candidate, and plan ahead are qualities that could really benefit you at home if they don't already. On the downside, things such as a tendency to procrastinate, less than stellar delegation skills, and a lack of attention to detail are all weaknesses that most likely make the occasional appearance at home.

Be candid about what you contribute to the office,

both the work that gets done and the culture of the company. Think about everything: your relationships with your teammates, your successes, your failures, promotions, client feedback, business that you've brought in, and circumstances where you've hired well or fired poorly.

We'll be honest: When we did this at home, the correlations between our work and home strengths and weaknesses was almost comical. Caitlin avoided uncomfortable conversations with her direct reports just as she avoided telling the babysitter to stop texting while putting the kids to bed. Andrew procrastinated logging in expenses both at home and at work. But it wasn't all bad news: We recognized that Andrew's attention to detail helps us with our ongoing lists and Caitlin's ability to multitask comes in handy when juggling the needs of the twins.

A Reminder

If you can't think of any specifics, then dig out your most recent job reviews to see what your supervisor has said about your work in the past. Caitlin pulled out a twelve-year-old review where her supervisor noted that she tended to over-commit to projects and then couldn't finish them on time. Now she would argue that this isn't true anymore and she has professionally matured, which is true. But occasionally there are situations where Caitlin takes on too much — organizing the twins' birthday parties in the middle of preparing for a major sales presentation at work — and ends up not being able to do it all. Meanwhile, Andrew once had a boss tell him that he tended to micromanage his employees, which crops up at home and leaves Caitlin feeling uncomfortably supervised.

Step back and take a hard look at your work persona and you might recognize areas where you are delivering at home and others where you're not. What we are shooting for here isn't perfection, because even the best coworker or boss is human, but what did you contribute to the team? Were you responsible, engaged, creative, a problem solver, generous with praise, supportive, reliable, loyal, energetic, and passionate? The best employees pull together the team and make the company a better place to be.

We want you to be this ideal colleague at home: to be the person that your partner can count on to deliver on promises, be engaged in the details of running a household, think big picture, offer solutions, be supportive, and help make your non-work life a happier one.

From the Desk of . . .

In 2003, Holly Bohn founded the stylish office supply online retailer See Jane Work. She sold her company in 2010 but continues to grow the business in her new role as creative director. She has young children, has a busy professional life, and successfully manages to frequently work from home. As someone who knows how to set up a home office better than anyone, we asked Holly to give us some tips for separating the work stuff from the home stuff.

For Those Who Are Space Challenged

Holly suggests that for those of you who don't have a dedicated office, you can use a "canvas tote or file box" to keep "frequently used files and office supplies" that you can pull out on your kitchen table or any other flat surface that can be used as a desk when you need it. If you don't have space for an entire room, then see if there is a corner in the family room or kitchen that you can claim. We have a friend who built a tiny office right under her stairs where she keeps their family calendar, chargers for electronic devices, bill caddy, and supplies. It's small but an efficient use of space.

For Those Who Have a Dedicated Home Office

First of all, consider yourself lucky that you have this much space. Holly suggests taking a little time to plan out the area by "being clear about exactly what storage you will need, what work surfaces you have, and who will be working in the space." Holly recommends a "large desk with a chair on one side and a bench on the other." Her kids sit on the bench doing their homework while she sits in the chair doing her paper-work. She emphasizes the importance of using a filing cabinet. "No matter how reliable your computer is and how many bills you pay online, you still need to file some paperwork," says Holly. While setting up your file cabinet, have a quick chat with your accountant and attorney about what family paperwork you should be keeping and what can be tossed.

Streamlining

Whether you have a home office box or a home office corner, Holly points out that you need a trash can and three letter trays—To Pay, To Do, To File—in the area where you sort your mail. Holly also suggests that you archive your files yearly and throw out "anything you can get online, including manuals."

Planning

For all of us, outside commitments can throw plan-ning out of balance. If you are traveling for business or there are a bunch of events happening in the school, this might impact your ability to balance work and personal responsibilities. Holly recommends setting aside a few minutes each morning to "take a sheet of paper and force yourself to write down your priorities

each day." She reminds us that although "every day
might not go as planned, it gives you the opportunity
to correct yourself and make sure you are being proac-
tive rather than reactive."

Your Family Culture

We've all heard about the importance of corporate culture
to a company's success, but what does that mean exactly?
Corporate culture is a synthesis of the behavior, values,
standards, attitudes, and styles that define the work being
done and shared at a company. The best companies have
the utmost respect for their employees. They set high but
achievable standards, offer training when needed, and demonstrate a commitment to their employees' professional
growth. The best companies also have the utmost respect
for their customers and clients and consistently deliver
great products that in turn can inspire the employee to
work harder and better.

The family culture is no different. As a unit you
embody values and standards that result in how things get
done at home, and in turn how you are perceived by the
world. Your culture defines how things are communicated
between you and the outside world, what you expect from

each other, rules and regulations like what's okay to say in front of the kids, how you treat your friends and family, and what is important for your family to participate in. We have friends who wanted their children to understand the importance of giving back. From a very young age, every Thanksgiving morning they would take their children to help out in a local food bank. We also know another family who maintains an open-door policy to their friends in need. They have put up friends who were out of jobs, needed a place to live, and were dealing with a breakup. Other couples we interviewed for this book believe in clean houses, living debt-free, and keeping in touch with distant relatives by sending out holiday cards. In our house one of our values is having strong friendships, so we host a dinner party or two each month.

So how would you define your family culture? Are your values reflected in how you are prioritizing things at home? For most of us, the answer to this would be "sometimes." Do we wish we were spending more time with our kids doing homework? *Yes.* Do we wish we were eating together more often as a family? *Yes.* So we can't do it all of the time, but we're finally at the point of knowing what is important to each of us and where we need to make some adjustments. Take it from us, if you and your partner aren't in agreement on your family culture, it can lead to tension and ongoing disagreements. Talking about what you want your family to be is an important discussion to have.

A Few Ways to Make
Family Time a Good Time

Once you've established issues and started setting your sights on goals, if you're like most of the people we interviewed, the priority is time—especially more time with family. We promise that we are going to help you get that time back. Here are some of the ways the couples we interviewed took moments to enjoy each other. We loved their suggestions and have spent the last year incorporating many of these into our week.

Don't Rush Breakfast

If you are anything like we were a year ago, breakfast is a ten-minute race. As the kids slurp down cold cereal, you run around stuffing the backpack, filling out permission slips, and making lunch. Remember this meal will set the tone for the day, so slow down! Get organized the night before, set the alarm a little earlier, and enjoy the morning meal. And if you find a little extra time after eating breakfast, find something fun to do together. Whenever there is a window of time in the morning and it isn't raining outside, Andrew takes our son to the park to throw the football for a few minutes before school. We've even found that the morning exercise helps our son concentrate better in class.

Eat Dinner Together

While it might not be possible to do this every night, try to commit to at least three or four dinners together a week. Eating dinner together provides a nice closure to the day. We spoke to one family who, because of work and various extracurricular commitments, doesn't get home until 6:30 p.m. They have all agreed that the kids need a break after getting home, so they will spend these nights doing the homework at the dinner table. They told us that it's not the time to foster great table manners, but it is a time where they can learn more about what the kids are working on and spend a little time decompressing after a busy day.

Give Yourselves at Least a Half Hour Before Jumping in on Homework

We interviewed a social worker involved in the public school system who said that many families jump into homework as soon as they open the front door. Not a good idea. Parents are tired, kids are tired, and no one wants to deal with homework. So give yourselves at least thirty minutes of personal time before diving in.

Try Educational Games Instead
of Watching Television

We used to come home exhausted from the day and let the kids watch television. The thirty minutes became an hour, and eventually we were squeezing in the homework between episodes of *iCarly*. Not good. A teacher suggested that for downtime we play a learning game like Scrabble or Bananagrams when we got home. The kids could then have downtime while still learning. Truth be told, we started looking forward to playing these games too.

Ask Questions Like "If you could
go anywhere in the world . . ."
and "My favorite meal includes . . ."

A family we interviewed for this book loves throwing out these types of questions while on a road trip, at a restaurant, or even when waiting in the dentist's office. We tried this and learned just how deep our daughter's obsession with Hawaii went—and she's never even been there.

Discover New Things Together: Restaurants, Stores, Museums, Streets, and Events

This holds true for families with kids and without. Going on adventures large and small is fun for everyone involved, but it takes a little planning and motivation. Instead of settling for the same old activities, go somewhere new.

Make Homework Fun

Seems impossible, right? *Nope.* We spoke to a school counselor who told us to pull out an egg timer to motivate the kids. She suggested that when their focus is off and they are "bored," set the timer for each assignment. We tried it with our son—ten minutes for the subtraction table—and he loved it. Not only did he buzz through the task, but he also enjoyed the challenge.

Cook Meals Together

Yes, after a long day at work, you might feel that supervising your child while you try to make dinner is a little much, but many (*many*) families we interviewed found this to be a fun way to bring everyone together. Try having your kids contribute to preparing meals by giving them tasks they can accomplish alone. This will build their confidence while also helping you out.

Tackle Big Projects as a Family

The garage needs cleaning, the lawn needs raking, or the bulbs need planting. Don't do it alone. Many hands will make the work easier and the time go by faster. Kids also love to feel as if they are contributing, so let them help you.

When it comes to doing anything as a family, remember to have realistic expectations about what people can contribute to, their stamina, and their interests. You can also get more out of each event by asking everyone for solutions and ideas.

2

"i thought you took care of that!"

JOB DESCRIPTIONS

Does this exchange sound familiar?

"Did you RSVP to Jim and Sharon's wedding?"

"No, I thought you did."

"Wasn't the deadline a week ago?"

"I don't know . . . I can't find the invitation."

How about this one?

"Did you call the insurance company about that bill
we need to dispute?"

"No."

"Oh, I thought you were going to do that."

"Can you do it? I'm swamped right now."

"Sure. Where's the bill?"

"You don't have it?"

Or this one?

> "We really should check in on Phil. He's not doing
>   very well."
> "I know, I was just thinking about him the other day.
>   We haven't talked to him since he got the news."

Since this book was inspired by an endless series of exchanges like these in our household, the topic of who is doing what is near and dear to our hearts. One of the great ironies of marriage can be that when you put two self-sufficient adults together, they are less on top of things as a pair than they are as individuals.

That sounds crazy, but when you think about it, it actually makes perfect sense. When you were single, you knew who was doing everything: *You were*. Now that you're part of a couple, one of two busy people who rely on each other, there's the potential for confusion. Plenty of potential. Several times a day. And if you add kids to the mix, then forget about it! Without some discussion or plan for who is doing what, there's almost nothing that isn't capable of slipping through the cracks.

As we've seen over and over again throughout our working lives, the same dynamic occurs in an office. When individual employees don't "own" certain tasks, things simply don't get done. But in an efficient office, everyone has a job description that defines his or her roles and responsibilities. (And the best thing about knowing your exact job is that you can cross *everything else* off your list.)

We'd be remiss if we didn't touch upon gender issues in this chapter, because as much as roles and responsibilities in society have changed, there are still rampant assumptions out there about what is a "girl job" and what is a "guy job," and they don't—or shouldn't—apply anymore. For instance, following a *Girl's Guide* book signing in Chicago, a woman approached Caitlin to talk about her feelings of being overwhelmed. No wonder she was stressed out: Not only was she a vice president at a major international shipping company, with a staff of more than one hundred employees, but she was also the mother of five children. Despite her enormous professional obligations, and the monster paycheck that came with them, her work-at-home husband still felt that it was her job to do the grocery shopping and cooking every single night! The irony is that the woman told Caitlin that her husband was actually the better cook and enjoyed food shopping more than she did.

To free yourself from such outdated models, it's important to create a schedule and division of labor that is fair and equitable. For example, the husband in the above example might be resistant to making dinner, but we bet that if he tried it a few times, he'd realize that it isn't that difficult to, say, take a few minutes out of his home-office day to pop a chicken in the oven, and, more than that, he would find that investing those few hours each week would pay enormous emotional dividends in how he and his wife relate to each other.

To start shaping your respective job descriptions, write down who currently does what in your household on a daily, weekly, monthly, and annual basis. Some of the jobs will inevitably be mundane (taking out the garbage, packing the kids' lunches), but we'll share our strategies for making those tasks more palatable by surrounding them with more rewarding work. Later, in "The Right Person for the Job," we'll explain how and why to assign tasks that are in line with each person's innate skills, interests, and passions. We'll also include tips on how to make chores as enjoyable as possible and how to incorporate fun tasks— such as researching or planning family activities and dates—that make the overall list more appealing. And we'll look at how to tell if the combined workload is too taxing, in which case you might need to scale back your ambitions or, if you can afford it, bring in some extra hands or ask for some help from family and friends.

In this chapter you'll find tips for how to have a job summit without storming away furious about how much more you do around the house, you'll get a therapist's take on whether or not fifty-fifty is even a realistic goal, and you'll find a helpful list of tasks to give to your kids. You'll hear from a couple who could obviously benefit enormously from creating and sticking to job descriptions. In addition, tips for how not to micromanage your partner are highlighted throughout this chapter, tips that will help you build an even stronger foundation at home.

What Needs to Get Done?

Before we can even step into figuring out who does what, we have to take a look at what really needs to get done in, around, and to the household and *when*. There are some tasks that you need to do once a day. Others only get taken care of once a year. So we are going to ask you to sit down and think in broad strokes about this list. Don't panic when you see what you've come up with. It's going to be long and daunting, but that's why we're all here—to make our lives more manageable.

Every Day

These tasks are the things that you often take care of without even thinking about them. The small actions that keep the household running are likely the tasks that you argue about the most: the mountain of laundry in the corner, the dishes in the sink, the piles of mail on the table that need sorting, and all of the everyday stuff that feels more overwhelming than it should. These are the chores we want you to add to the list, because when these are taken care of, the clutter-free *physical space* will give you some clutter-free *mental space* to attend to the bigger things that need to be accomplished.

You might consider adding:

- Laundry (with kids, this can be a daily chore!)
- Washing dishes and putting them away
- Making breakfast, lunch, and dinner
- Setting and clearing the table
- Sorting the mail
- Tidying up the house
- Walking the dog
- Feeding and cleaning up after the pets
- Packing lunches
- Making the bed(s)
- Doing homework with the kids
- Dropping the kids off at school/picking them up from school
- Collecting, sorting, and taking out garbage

Weekly

These are the to-dos that you most often leave to the weekend because you have considerably more time than you do during the week to get on top of them. Remember that later we'll show you how to tackle these more efficiently and more quickly, because, let's face it, the weekend is your opportunity for downtime and none of us want to spend the entire time on chores.

You might consider adding:

- Gardening and yard work
- Deep-cleaning the house
- Paying the bills and banking
- Home repairs
- Food shopping
- Replacing broken household items
- Coordinating kid activities (games, playdates, homework, parties, orthodontist)
- Reviewing and booking child care
- Going to the dump and/or recycling center
- Putting gas in the car

Monthly/Seasonally

These are the jobs that crop up throughout the year that can't really be planned for on a weekly basis. They are the tasks you don't have to think about daily or even weekly, but they can't be forgotten.

You might consider:

- Taking care of the car (tune-ups, changing the oil)
- Planning for upcoming vacations

- Seasonal changes to the house (installing storm windows/air conditioners, shutting down/opening up pools)
- Major cleaning projects (basement, garage, attic)
- Spring/fall yard cleanup
- Updating budget
- Scheduling doctor and dentist visits
- Reconciling the bank accounts
- Buying kids' clothes (back-to-school, winter coats, camp, etc.)
- Pet grooming and vet visits
- Camp registration and scheduling after-school lessons and sports
- Picking up birthday presents

Yearly

These are some of the bigger tasks that, even though you only attend to them once a year, are crucial to your keeping everything on track.

You might consider adding:

- Annual checkups
- Taxes
- Car registration
- Home renovations
- Holiday planning (gifts, parties, travel)

These are only suggestions, and we're sure there are many that we forgot to include. Take a walk through your house, flip through the calendar, and review the bills to see what else needs to be attended to in your household.

Job Summit

You have now created a somewhat comprehensive list of what it takes to run your household and family. It's a long list as it is, and we didn't even ask you to break up the big jobs (laundry) into all of their components (washing, drying, folding, putting away). It's mostly daunting because running the household is actually your second job. You have a full to-do list at work that you are responsible for before you come home to this one. So why is the one at work so much easier to look at? Because at work you know exactly what you need to do, what your direct reports need to do, and what your coworkers need to do. There is less drama, less assumption, and less arguing at work, in part because roles and responsibilities are clearly defined. Not so at home. This is to everyone's detriment, because it would relieve a lot of tension and pressure if we all knew exactly what was expected of us . . . and if it was an even distribution of labor. So take a good, hard look at the lists you have created and write down who is currently doing what.

Please note that we know that this exercise has the potential to get ugly, but we are asking you not to let it. If you are like most people, you focused on what the other person is *not* doing around the house. We're guessing that when you were working on the lists above in your mind, you were saying things like, "Yep, I do that too and this one and this one . . ." Anytime you shed light on how a household runs, you will see that the division of labor is rarely even close to fifty-fifty. This isn't the fault of one person or the other, because it's very easy to let roles and responsibilities be assumed without a conversation, and it can happen gradually and without a discussion. All of a sudden you are the person making dinner every night, which was fine when you didn't have kids and other things to do in the evening, such as helping out with homework, filling out permission forms, and putting the kids to bed.

Yes, there is anger and frustration inherent in this issue of who does what for the household, but the only way this can get readjusted is to own that you were complacent in this situation and commit to changing it. Is it even? Most likely not. But let it go. That was then, this is now, and we are starting with a clean slate. Look at this list again in a week, once the distribution is even, so that you can feel good about it.

From the Desk of . . .

Because we know firsthand how potentially volatile it can be to redefine our roles at home, we spoke to therapist and author Linda Brierty about how to best navigate these conversations.

Is Fifty-Fifty Even Attainable?

According to Linda, "It is impossible to have a perfectly equal division of labor in family life. A general sense of each person pulling their own weight is a more reasonable goal." She believes, as we we do, that "being reactive and defensive is a major communication obstacle for many couples, leading to arguments that obscure the actual issues."

But what about when the tensions over who is doing what are rising? "Ever an idealist, I like to put couples on an anger detox program, where fighting is actually not an option. So often we think it is an acceptable way to engage with each other. It actually erodes the romantic element of the relationship and becomes a repetitive pattern. It is destructive rather than constructive."

Communication as Conversation

Linda advises that whenever issues arise, "couples practice respectful, direct communication with an eye toward conflict resolution and what is called 'working through' problems." Linda assured us that "there will be less avoidance when couples don't fear an angry, volatile interchange." Many of us dread conflict and confrontation so much that we will take on extra responsibilities in order to avoid it. Linda suggests, "Why don't you think of it as communication and conversation instead?" If you've tried your best and it just isn't possible to have a conversation that doesn't escalate into an argument, then we recommend giving it a rest for now. Take a walk. Visit friends. Try again some other time.

Show Some Appreciation, People!

Since you are now going to do things differently, we want you to start with recognizing the work that the other person is putting into the home. Linda reminds us that "it can be incredibly rewarding to feel that you have an equal partner in life, both working toward the same goals and supporting each other. A good dose of appreciation for what the other is doing is always recommended." Linda believes that "daily kindness and appreciation are essential to help face the challenges in life. Ideally, home is a sanctuary where we find peace and restore ourselves. The emotional tone of the home is very important, and of course children pick up on that as well."

There Is Nothing Good About Micromanaging

There isn't anyone who thrives when being micromanaged, especially at home. Linda agrees and says, "Micromanaging each other is insulting and ultimately self-defeating. It provokes anger and is disempowering." Just think about how it makes you feel when your boss tells you to redo a tiny, insignificant task, just because you didn't do it exactly as he would have. Now at home, who wants to be redirected on how to fold laundry, put dishes in the dishwasher, or pack a school lunch? Linda says, "It is often a disincentive for people, who may then become passive-aggressive and stop doing things entirely. Then the power struggles and ego games begin." The end result is that less gets done around the house, and the person micromanaging will often get stuck with more of the work.

Getting Past Outdated Roles

Now that working couples are more common than not, we need to adjust the way we think about home. Linda feels that now is "a perfect time to step out of outdated patriarchal assumptions, behaviors, and institutions to embrace equality. I know many men who embrace parenting and taking care of a home, many women who need to go to work to fulfill their identity, and many who do a combination of both. The couple can see each other as they are and allow their true selves to blossom, without any prescribed roles." We couldn't agree more.

Why It Shouldn't Be "All Business"

Because we all struggle with finding time for one another, we spoke to Linda about the key to keeping romance alive in the face of overwhelming family responsibilities. "We have all heard about date night, and yes, it is so important to get dressed up and get out of the house. However, I don't feel that that is enough if the rest of the time the couple is fighting about chores." So what is the key? "I think that having a pragmatic, businesslike approach to the business aspects of family life is healthy. It will keep the emotions in check and prevent the daily details from corrupting the relationship. The couple needs to be mindful, though, not to make the whole relationship about work. This is a common trap. Spend time together that is not 'productive.' Being with each other without a task is essential. Being together without excessive social engagements is also important. Work and overbooking can be a defense against intimacy, so maintaining the romance is also a safeguard against partners trying to get their needs met outside of the relationship."

Changing Roles Can Change Your Relationship . . . for the Better

You want to do things differently at home, but there may be conflicts that arise while working toward that goal. Linda recommends keeping in mind that "as you implement the changes you are seeking, there will naturally be some type of transformation that occurs in the relationship." In some cases there will be resistance, but you are defining your relationship and your home together, so if it needs to be done differently to suit the needs of both of you, so be it. Linda reminds us that if something isn't working for you, speak up, take a stand, and find solutions together.

The Right Person for the Job

You have come up with the big ol' list, you've discussed it with your partner, and you have most likely realized that some adjustments need to happen. At this
point, to get us all on the right path, we need to start from
scratch, throwing out the roles based on gender assumptions and all of the other determining factors that came
before now.

When determining job responsibilities, it's best to start
with what you enjoy. If you're really lucky, then your partner's strengths and interests are not the same as yours
(hey, opposites attract, right?), in which case assigning
tasks will be painless. For example, if you love to drive
alone, relishing the fact that you can blast the Beastie Boys
with no eye rolling from anyone, then maybe you should
take on a chore such as going to the grocery store. Maybe
your partner likes to be outdoors on the weekends, or
needs to find a more convenient source of exercise than
the gym she never gets to, in which case she is the logical
candidate for gardening and lawn mowing. There are
countless factors that might influence your own job
descriptions. The point is that to take on responsibilities
that fit, you should start with playing to your strengths
and what you like to do.

Here are some possible matchmaking tips:

If you like to . . .	you might consider taking on:
organize	paying bills, cleaning out closets, filing receipts, being the liaison with the accountant
make phone calls	scheduling appointments, making social plans, disputing bills
drive	errands such as a trip to the garden store
clean	keeping the house, the garage, and/or the car tidy
plan	meals, long-term finances
shop	selecting and purchasing gifts, household decorations, and groceries
be outside	gardening, washing the car

We learned that it will be impossible for the list of responsibilities to be split fifty-fifty, but just as at work, if most of the tasks are aligned with your skills and interests, then it shouldn't be as painful for either of you to take chores on. Chances are also pretty good that you can do things more quickly if they are in your comfort zone. For instance, at work Caitlin struggles with creating profit and loss statements and relies heavily on the finance team to do it with her, so imagine the potential for disaster if it were Caitlin's job at home to balance the budgets and work alone on the financial forecasts. Truth be told, this was her responsibility for a few years and it did lead to a few heart-stopping moments. The point is that while everything on your list can't fall into the category of what you like to do, work together to split it up more along the lines of what you do well.

A True Story: Recipe for Disaster

Hailey and James are a working couple in New York City. She's the financial director of a major magazine and he's a restaurant chef. They don't have specific jobs defined at home, instead "taking on tasks based on who has more time that day, week, etc. We consider time constraints and respective work pressures. . . . In general, we kind of figure it out as things come along and don't have any formal recurring assignments." Hailey then adds, "Which may be part of why we don't get as much done as we'd like!"

We couldn't have said it better ourselves, because things don't just happen. Do you think that your office just cleans itself, that assignments just get done without some conversation and planning? Any kind of work, either at home or in the office, requires a little engagement from the participants. Hailey tells us that James works at night, so he is generally free during the day. What a great opportunity to take care of errands that might involve long lines on weekends, like buying clothes for their daughter, grocery shopping, and going to the post office.

Building Tension

Hailey explains that "we seem to discuss chores when they don't get done!" and "I remind James more and more frequently when he is not up to date on birthdays and other family occasions that I have not taken on myself. Although this doesn't seem to be working very well."

These two need to take a step back, because Hailey shouldn't have to remind James to do anything and if things aren't getting done, clearly she gets angry. What these two need is to create a to-do list, split it up, and let each other be. They would really benefit from the advice we offer in the following chapter on having weekly meetings.

Please—No Micromanaging

James and Hailey have very different thresholds for dirty laundry. "He can't abide a full hamper and I can," laments Hailey. So James ends up doing the laundry most of the time, though he freely admits to wishing she would take the initiative more often. For the same reason, Hailey has become used to James doing a lot of the household cleaning. "I am sometimes dissatisfied with his standards on a particular task," though she adds, "James does so much around the house that it seems wrong for me to criticize."

Just as you respect the individuality of your colleagues at work, so should you respect the individuality of your partner. If James has an issue with the laundry and is willing to take on that task, then make it part of his job description. If Hailey feels strongly about the quality of James's housecleaning, she can either take it on as part of her job description or just let it go. You can't start micromanaging your partner: he is not your employee. If there is lingering tension over who does what and how, then in their job summit, James and Hailey can air their respective concerns, James explaining that he wishes Hailey would do more laundry and Hailey explaining that she is sometimes dissatisfied with his standards on other chores. We can't make their decisions for them, but it seems that the easy, equitable solution is for James to simply take on the laundry on a weekly basis (or more often, if necessary) and for Hailey to take on those tasks that she wishes were done to perfection. That way, everybody gets what they feel is important (an empty hamper for James; well-scrubbed floors and sinks for Hailey), and there's no ambiguity as to who's doing what.

Playing to Strengths

Okay, on to bigger and more time-consuming items. When it comes to the family's financial and administrative maintenance, Hailey explains: "My gut reaction to this is that I notice more, but it does depend on the area. . . . I'm more aware of tasks/projects related to our daughter, and to overall administration and finance such as insurance, money, investments, doctor's visits, purchases, etc. In general, I would say that I am more aware than James of all the things we need to take care of—I have a good memory, and am more of a worrier—but I do not take over execution, partly because James is a better executor. I think of all the things that have to get done and set priorities, etc., but James handles the actual doing of them more than I do these days. He is very organized and methodical, and gets stuff done!"

Hailey and James have job descriptions on several fronts, though they don't know it. In effect, Hailey is the family's chief financial officer, with the vision and responsibility for monitoring what needs to happen, and James is the administrator, the person who executes what needs to be done. Now, just think how efficient these two would be if they made these jobs formal and set a monthly time to go over all those tasks, rather than attacking them as they pop into mind. And just think about how much mental energy Hailey would free up by not needing to be the "worrier."

Ten Reasons It Is Essential to Relax

With a million things going on every day, relaxing seems like a pipe dream. But from what we have learned personally and from all of the experts we interviewed, it is crucial for your well-being and the well-being of your family to have a period of time each day to relax.

Here is a list of the top ten reasons that finding downtime is essential.

1. You will be open to new ideas and points of view.
2. You will have the ability to think about the big picture of your lives together.
3. You will be healthier.
4. You will have more energy.
5. You will be more focused, which will make you more efficient.
6. You will have the bandwidth to appreciate the other person.
7. You won't feel as angry.
8. You will be able to let go of things and forgive more quickly.
9. You will have a better sleep schedule.
10. You will have a better memory.

Your Job Shouldn't Be a Drag at the Office or at Home

Come on . . . there are a few chores on the list that you secretly enjoy, like the quiet drive to the supermarket when you get to listen to whatever music you want without grief, and the physical satisfaction you get out of raking the autumn leaves. But even the tasks that are a drag, like taking out the garbage, can be painless with the right attitude. What that right attitude is may be is entirely personal. For some a chore becomes more pleasant if it's done in the shortest time possible; for others, doing it well makes the difference. Whatever motivates you at work will most likely motivate you at home. If you are at your office looking at a long list of projects that you don't enjoy, how do you get through it? Do you pick your most efficient time of day to tackle the hardest task? Do you listen to music at your desk when having to review endless profit and loss statements? We recently read an article in *The Wall Street Journal* that found that many executives play music before tough meetings to get them mentally prepared. There are also tasks on that to-do list that you might actually enjoy, such as shopping for new clothes for the kids, swapping the winter coats for bathing suits, or planning for the holidays.

There are also opportunities on your to-do list to bond with your partner or children. At work when your team works together to brainstorm, strategize, and plan, there is a strengthening of the professional relationships going on at the same time. You know the feeling when you leave a really productive and satisfying collective brainstorming session. It feels good; it feels like you are in it together and that you solved a problem or discovered a big idea. You can have this same feeling at home if you and your partner take on certain tasks jointly. For instance, wouldn't it feel good to sit down with your partner and plan the next family vacation? Or take a few hours together to discuss a major goal like buying a new house? Even the small stuff, like cleaning out the garage, offers an opportunity for bonding. The point is that you don't need to take the list and go off on your own all the time. Accomplish some of the fun stuff together. Before you know it, you could actually look forward to getting things done.

Tasks for Kids

Kids need job descriptions too! This might sound slightly curmudgeonly, but after the last ten years of managing the next generation, Caitlin feels strongly that the level of entitlement in the workplace has reached an all-time high. And we are guessing you have experienced the same. Have you encountered potential employees that ask about vacation time during the first interview? The new employee who pushes back on the entry-level tasks? The recently promoted assistant who wants to go from cube to windowed office? We're not sure about you, but we want our kids to enter the workforce with both confidence and a willingness to be part of a team, so we hope that by bringing our own kids into the "who does what" discussion, we will put them on the right path. Not because we want you to start thinking of your kids as potential employees, but because having them contribute to the household work helps everyone. Responsibilities help children mature and build confidence. They will feel a part of what is happening at home, will learn to take ownership of their own to-do list, and will feel good about themselves when you praise them for getting it all done. Having your kids take on jobs will also help lighten your load. We heard a relative talking recently about how, when he was a teenager, his mother would still pick up his room and clean up after him at the dining-room table. Yikes! Who has time for that?

We want to encourage you to bring your kids into the household tasks as early as possible, even if it's something small like putting their toys away. (Actually, that isn't always small.) We want this generation to have an appreciation of responsibility and hard work, right? What better way than to teach them to contribute at home?

Jobs for the Three- to Five-Year-Old

- Put away the toys.
- Put clothes in the hamper.
- Set the table (except, perhaps, for the knives).

Jobs for the Six- to Eight-Year-Old

- Clear the table.
- Hang up the backpacks.
- Feed the pets.
- Hang up the coats and put away the shoes.
- Pick up the bathroom after a shower/bath.
- Make the bed (it doesn't have to be perfect!)

Jobs for the Nine- to Twelve-Year-Old

- Fold and put away the laundry.
- Make breakfast.
- Help with dinner.
- Put out the garbage.
- Collect the recycling.
- Pack lunch.
- Empty the dishwasher.
- Lay out clothes for the next morning.
- Water the plants.

Jobs for Thirteen-Year-Olds and Older

- Rake the leaves; help with the garden.
- Mow the lawn.

- Clean out the garage.
- Babysit.
- Help clean the house.
- Walk the dogs.
- Prepare simple meals.
- Pack the lunch box.

From the Desk of . . .

Lori Hiller, LCSW, has a college degree in developmental psychology and a master's in social work. After ten years working at an outpatient mental health center for children and adolescents, she took her current position as an elementary school social worker. We spoke to Lori about giving children jobs around the house and the importance of bringing them into family planning.

Getting Kids to Work

Lori tells us that children "need to feel a sense of ownership and care for their home." Since it's important to start good habits young, teach toddlers to help you put away their toys.

To Pay or Not to Pay?

Lori feels strongly that "allowance and jobs should be directly linked" but that children shouldn't get paid for everything. Parents can use money for leverage, and extra-hard jobs such as raking, shoveling, or babysitting for a long period of time might be paid, but it's important that "children should do their jobs because they are part of a family and everyone in the family has responsibilities."

When Kids Should Be in the Loop

Although having kids sit in on every family discussion isn't necessary, "children can attend these meetings for short periods of time as soon as they start school." Once they're in school, children have both jobs and a schedule, so it's important for them to know that these are part of whatever else is happening at home."

Taking off her professional hat for a moment, Lori told us that "as a parent, I want my children to go off to college as independent students who can keep their things neat and clean and eventually cook for themselves and share a place to live . . . that is my goal and as they get older I teach them more skills to do that."

A True Story: These Two Have
It Figured Out

Rob and Averitt are newly engaged and have been living together for more than four years. A busy working couple with two households and a pet to take care of, they have a lot to juggle. Because Rob and Averitt manage a household without falling into the gender traps many of us contend with, we spoke to each of them about how decisions get made regarding who does what and how compromises are reached and expectations are set. What surprised us when we reread their interview was not only the fact that they seem entirely on the same page about who does what and why, but also on how drama-free the division of labor seems to be. Yes, they are able to afford a housekeeper and they don't have kids, but we know firsthand that these two have incredibly demanding professional lives and a commitment to various nonprofits that take plenty of time and energy.

Who Does What?

Averitt tells us that they don't have a formal division of responsibilities because they have a good balance around the house. "Each of us knows that the other is always working to keep things running smoothly and neither of us will walk past something that needs to be done." These two don't ignore something because it's the other person's job. Averitt uses coffee as an example. "Whoever wakes up first will make a pot of coffee and, although it's never been discussed, whoever didn't make the coffee will clear the cups and wash the pot." In this household they each unload the dishwasher, make the bed, and wash laundry when it needs doing. That being said, they "are each better at certain things and enjoy doing certain tasks more than the other," so roles and responsibilities are divided along those lines. "Rob is very good at fixing technical things like cable and Internet router glitches and electrical wiring problems, all of which just frustrate me," says Averitt. Averitt, on the other hand, "generally takes the lead on keeping everything organized, stocked, and ready in the house as well as for the lawn, and at keeping tabs on where we are supposed to be and when." According to Averitt, each of them trusts that the other is always pulling his or her own weight around the house.

Rob confirms that "household jobs get split up based largely on interest and skill, but time and a belief in variety sometimes change this." Rob tells us that he "lived in New York with a weekend home for many years and had become both proficient and interested in certain household jobs, including cooking to entertain, yard work, organizing social events and obligations, major food and provision shopping (i.e., Costco runs, wine purchases), and arranging service providers and contractors." He confesses that he "was not so good at some basics: household cleaning (for which we engage housekeepers, but which still requires some attention), laundry, watering plants, among others." Luckily, Averitt pays greater attention to detail and has a greater sense of pride about these jobs. According to Rob, Averitt is also "a better chef for the dinners we have on our own (more creative and motivated) and does a better job keeping our shared calendar (even though I am more active in initially arranging our social events)."

Take on as many tasks that suit your skills as possible and don't keep track of how much the other person is doing. We think that what makes it work for Averitt and Rob is that they've achieved the ideal balance between complementary skills and interests. They told us that they do the bigger household projects, like yard work, together and collaborate seamlessly on fun tasks such as entertaining. Like all of their household jobs, they didn't have a formal discussion about who does what, but it got divided up naturally.

Living Micromanagement-Free

Averitt believes that they are both good "at letting the other complete whatever task he or she has assumed and only offering advice if asked for." But beyond not stepping in to redirect, Averitt tells us that they have accepted each other's quirks. "Rob often likes things cut/chopped a certain way in the kitchen, I like towels and shirts folded a certain way in the laundry room, but each of us knows that about the other, understands that we also have our own quirks, and therefore it is rarely an issue."

Rob agrees that they don't micromanage each other, but they do occasionally ask each other if something has been done for which they are responsible. But he thinks this is "neither micromanaging nor nagging; I think it comes from a place of both guilt and gratitude that the other person has taken on that responsibility, and an anxiety that if something hasn't yet been done, maybe it would be fair to share that role (at least that one time)."

Accepting each other's quirks isn't always easy, but it is essential to living harmoniously. Your partner will not do things exactly the way you would do them, nor will they always do them when you would do them. Letting each of you have your own style and approach to the to-do list will help ease tension in your household.

Letting the Other Person Do His Thing

Averitt believes the key to their success is that they are "open to doing whatever tasks need to be done and never point the finger at the other to say that he or she is overstepping his responsibilities or not doing enough."

Rob trusts that their "shared values, complementary interests from the beginning, and now four-plus years of running two households together" offer them a pretty good understanding of what each of them should do and most likely has already done around the house.

Assume the other person is doing their best and let go of feeling defensive when the other person is checking in. It's important to go into this new phase trusting your partner. If your partner says she is going to do something, then believe she is going to do it.

Workplace Skills at Home

Averitt agrees that there is crossover between your work and home responsibilities.

"I think compromising, planning, and delegating all play important roles in keeping things running at home." As with most of us, Averitt and Rob have a busy workweek packed with job-related and social responsibilities that compress the amount of time they can spend on household tasks. They, like all of us, have to compromise on what can be accomplished and when it can be done, but looking at how businesses run can help. "Planning and organizing can make everything run much more smoothly and efficiently," says Averitt.

Rob brings a lot of the office home. His household tasks "reflect, without a doubt, certain professional skills:

Executive management and planning skills help me make social obligations and plan events; strategy and prioritization skills help me articulate travel options and the logistics of two households, and communications skills help with all the above."

Don't forget the skills you use at work. They are invaluable when applied to your home. Sure, you may still be unable to complete everything that needs to get done at home, but incorporating those professional skills, such as organization and delegating, will make your life a lot easier.

Working Through Conflict

Averitt acknowledges that setbacks are frustrating for everyone, but he "can't recall either one of us ever blaming the other for something running afoul or not getting completed." Averitt and Rob "genuinely believe that the other is doing his best to make things run smoothly and to see that all chores are completed." Therefore, if something isn't getting done, they approach the topic as a problem to solve, figuring out together how to avoid a similar pitfall in the future. They wisely believe that "blaming won't solve a problem; it'll only add to the stress and frustration."

Rob says that conflicts between them "typically arise when we simply have too much to do or something unexpected has arisen," so oftentimes the other person in the partnership will take on more household jobs in the short term.

We agree with Averitt and Rob that it helps everyone to try to be flexible about your workload, because unexpected things do crop up during the week. Also, being a good team member means being aware about what is on the other person's plate.

List Crazy

Averitt and Rob love lists more than almost anyone else we know. Averitt tells us that he and Rob "both write lists constantly, and on Saturday mornings over coffee or breakfast, we generally brainstorm on one comprehensive list that includes household projects, errands, social commitments, etc., and then both work off that one list, which sits out on the kitchen counter over the course of the weekend. A handwritten list sitting out for each of us to read is our best way to stay organized and focused." During the week they exchange one or two e-mails that detail their calendar and upcoming plans, which get added to their list.

We share the love of the list. In the next chapter you will learn how we use it as the basis for our weekly meetings.

putting it to paper

THE WEEKEND MEETING

Any successful professional team, big or small, has a regular meeting. It might take place weekly or monthly, or it might happen periodically out of necessity. There are the great meetings where we walk away having learned something new and feel inspired, motivated, and excited to jump in on an assignment. Then there are the meetings that are a complete waste of time because the agenda wasn't thought out or communicated in any helpful way.

As we shared in the introduction, we are former coworkers who witnessed how a good meeting can keep everyone focused and positive. It was on one fateful Saturday morning that we discovered that conducting our own meeting at home was the key to getting a handle on the details of our personal lives. Because we know firsthand that this works, we strongly believe that for any couple, a weekend meeting is essential to managing the minutiae of day-to-day life. More important, it keeps you on top of the small steps that will allow you to achieve big goals. In truth, a weekend meeting doesn't even have to be on a weekend. All you need is a small window of time—about thirty minutes—to focus on the details of your life together. We think that's a pretty small commitment to make for peace, structure, and the direction it can bring to your relationship. It's a time for assessing what's getting done, identifying what needs doing, and devising a plan for making it all happen. It's also a way of making sure that you are both taking on an equal amount of work.

This chapter will begin with the wide range of topics you may cover in your weekly meeting, including home maintenance and repairs, scheduling, finances and budget, shopping and meal planning, cleaning, organizing, paperwork, socializing, short- and long-term goals, and—if you have kids—all of their (numerous) activities and responsibilities. You might be shocked by how many things you come up with for your initial list, but don't be intimidated. Most likely, you won't be talking about every single action item each week.

While topics and logistics of the meeting can be flexible, there are five essential elements to making it work: planning, agenda, discussion, assigning, and recording. This chapter will discuss each one and cover the basics of a productive meeting, such as coming prepared and being honest and respectful of each other. We'll encourage you to be realistic about how much time you have each week and demonstrate how larger tasks can be broken up into smaller steps, perhaps over a span of weeks or months if necessary.

This chapter highlights an interview with a principal at a branding company who will offer advice for holding a productive meeting, sample agendas, and topics to help you create your own structure for the get-together, as well as the true story of a couple that discovered the benefits of bringing the office home when they launched a business together.

Why Have a Meeting?

We all know how insanely busy life is these days. Keeping up with the basic to-do list—buying groceries, making dinner, paying bills—is a challenge, never mind all of the other things we have to do each week, month, and year. And then there is splitting up the list with your partner, tracking what is getting done, assigning budgets to everything, making plans, confirming appointments. Even after one's roles have been divvied up, it's all a little insane—okay, a lot insane.

So why a meeting?

Because your household deserves your time, attention, and, most of all, focus. Laundry, shopping, cleaning, and organizing are all tasks that don't just happen. They require time, energy, planning, and a little thought. If you are like us, you're too busy to do everything on the fly. In fact, whenever we've left things to the very last minute, something inevitably falls through the cracks. And that *something* can be little and fixable—like forgetting to pick up milk on the way home—or *something* really big and unfixable—like forgetting a family member's birthday.

Think we are overstating the importance of family meetings? Imagine how your office would run without any meetings. You wouldn't have any idea what your colleagues are working on, what needs to be accomplished, or even how the company is doing. Without meetings at the office, you could neither delegate to the people who work for you nor could you be given work. A company without meetings is a group of people sharing an office while not communicating. Meetings are as essential to home life as they are to work life. If you don't spend time catching up with your partner, reviewing the list of what needs to get done, or making future plans, then you are setting yourself up for disagreements, resentment, and a series of ill-informed decisions.

Of everything we ask you to tackle in this book, having a meeting is the easiest to commit to and offers the most rewards. Just consider for a moment how much you can get done in an hour—jobs for the week assigned, an action plan for the holidays finished, babysitter for

Saturday hired, bills paid, budget for upcoming vacation figured out. We would even argue that taking that one hour to sit down, review everything that needs to get done that week (or even month), and actually talking about it will save you from hours of arguments and multiple misunderstandings.

So there is our last pitch for why your family should have a meeting. Have we sold you? If not, read on anyway!

The Office Meeting

If you are like most professionals, you sit in on a number of meetings that are a complete waste of time. You know, the ones where nothing new gets said; problems go unresolved; there is too much covering of one's ass and too little offering up of solutions; there is no big-picture thinking, direction, or focus. Chances are good that the majority of the meetings you attend go like that. *But* there are the great meetings, where the group is fixing problems, sharing new ideas, figuring out better ways to do things, identifying ways to make or save money, supporting one another's work. These are the meetings that people leave thinking, "I'm glad I'm at this company."

The good meetings don't just happen; someone took the time to prepare for them. Thought was put into what topics would be covered when the agenda was created. Care was taken to send everyone reading materials prior to the meeting so that you were all on the same page. Someone managed the flow of the conversation, notes were taken, next steps assigned. These good meetings are the ones that move the company forward and bring the employees together, where everyone leaves knowing their next steps.

Start paying attention to how meetings are run at your company. Are there things that you can take home? Caitlin had a former boss who insisted that whoever called a meeting was responsible for creating and distributing an agenda at least a day beforehand. This was incredibly helpful for the attendees, who then had time to prepare their contributions to the meeting. Andrew worked for someone who would recap what was covered at the end of each team meeting, assigning tasks and answering any lingering questions along the way. This gave everyone a clear sense of what was expected of him or her. Unfortunately, you also may notice bad habits and behaviors that you do not want to bring home. Caitlin has had managers who refused to delegate specific action items during a meeting, leaving the team confused about who was responsible for what.

List Basics

Keep your weekly list to those tasks that you can get done within the week. You can move forward to bigger goals, such as renovating the kitchen, by breaking that project down into steps—setting a budget, researching a contractor, reviewing designs, scheduling construction work—adding one or two of those steps to the upcoming weekly lists. If you add action items that are too big and take too many steps to actually get done within the course of a week, you'll find that you won't be crossing much off the list.

Don't go crazy on the list itself. There is really only so much you can do each week. So be prudent about how much you put on it. Try to keep it to one page. Before committing to getting it all done, look at the week ahead.

For those tasks that you absolutely hate doing, try setting a time limit for getting them done. Clean the bathrooms: fifteen minutes. Mop the basement floor: ten minutes. You get the idea. If you look down at something you really don't want to do, we also recommend that you do it first.

If you have tasks on your list that need to get done early in the week, move those up to the top of the list, noting the due date. It is helpful when you are planning out your week to know what you need to focus on first.

Group the to-dos so when you are looking down at the list during a lunch break, you can see the four tasks you can get done from your desk. Our groups include *calls* (appointments we need to make, reservations we need to cancel, bills we need to question), *errands* (packages we need to bring to the post office, dry cleaning we need to pick up, library books we need to return), *shopping* (we split this further into food, hardware, pet store, gifts), and *kids* (set up playdates, sign them up for camp).

Once you have created the list, then pull out the calendars—either the shared calendar or your own—and start adding the tasks to your upcoming schedule. Looking at your schedule and knowing that you are taking both lunch hours on Wednesday and Thursday to knock out the planning for your mother's big birthday party will put your mind at ease when it feels like the date is imminent.

A final note about lists: Create them together based on what you decided needed to get done in the weekly meeting. Writing the to-do lists together makes sure that nothing will be forgotten and you will both be able to see if the tasks are evenly distributed.

True Story: The Power of a Meeting

Justine and Nick have been married for eight years. Busy working parents of two young girls, they stumbled upon the benefits of having a weekly meeting in the middle of a particularly stressful period.

We spoke to Justine and Nick about how they touch base on the very long list of things that need to get done to keep their home and family running smoothly. These are the lessons they offer.

Transform Cranky Exhaustion into a Breakfast Date

During a busy home-renovation project, Justine and Nick were having a serious communication breakdown. After working all morning and doing the mom thing with their two preschoolers in the afternoon, Justine ended the day with barely enough energy to get through the latest issue of *Entertainment Weekly*. Her husband, meanwhile, seeing her reclining on the couch at night, figured it was the perfect time to look at possible bathroom fixtures online. Needless to say, arguments ensued. "This tension went on sporadically for a few weeks before a lightbulb went on over my head," said Justine. She suggested that they hold periodic "house meetings" over breakfast at a local restaurant instead of at night when they "risked cranky exhaustion."

We have had very similar miscommunications in our household. Once the kids have been fed and put to bed, Andrew likes to jump into the to-do list, taking advantage of the quiet. Caitlin wants to take advantage of the quiet . . . by watching television. So like Justine and Nick, they agreed to have the catch-up while cleaning up after dinner and the more detailed weekly meeting on Saturday afternoon. The point is that you need to pick a time to connect on the household details that works for both of you.

Get Past the Same Old Argument

All couples have their "trouble spots," those issues that form the theme for the bulk of their arguments. Fortunately, more often than not, it takes just a few simple adjustments in the way things are approached or talked about to clear things up. In Justine and Nick's case the trouble spot was "differing opinions on the urgency of any given matter." What seemed time-sensitive to Nick registered very low on Justine's priority list. Meanwhile, Justine would send Nick e-mails asking him to do things, and they would promptly get lost among the hundreds of incoming messages he receives each day in his job. Since things weren't moving quickly enough for either of them, both Justine and Nick felt like their needs weren't important to the other. The end result was that the bulk of their exchanges became nagging in nature.

Their solution to improving this cycle of inadvertent badgering was, once again, found in the meeting. "The opportunity to sit down and not only dole out assignments, but make sure prioritization and timelines are laid out, helps to avoid any undercurrent of suggestion that one didn't make time for the other's request," says Justine. Once they hit on this solution, Justine stopped sending nonurgent e-mails about household issues, Nick stopped interrupting Justine's precious evening downtime with renovation concerns, and they both began keeping running lists in their own notebooks until they could review them together during their meeting.

Justine and Nick are right about the importance of setting deadlines when assigning the weekly to-dos. You both need to be on the same page about when things are going to get done, because, as they discovered, your timeline might be very different from your partner's.

No More Double Booking

Like many of us trying to keep multiple balls in the air, Justine and Nick often had those "I told you about this four weeks ago!" moments. Their solution? The weekly calendar swap. "We highlight items we want to make sure the other knows about (e.g., who won't be home for dinner on this night, who has a business trip) and we write in questions that need to be answered (e.g., Can you come home early on that night?)." Justine and Nick make sure to review the calendar during their weekly meeting and add appointments and obligations to a shared calendar posted in the kitchen.

We've incorporated reviewing calendars into our weekly meeting as well, because commitments can often impact the household schedule. Don't forget to also review your kids' calendars, school calendars, and the calendars of your child care provider if you have one.

Figure Out Who Does What

We all know that the goal of a household meeting is to divide and conquer the household to-do list, but how do you decide who does what? Justine and Nick told us that they generate assignments based on "what makes more sense" and "who cares more that it gets done." Nick takes on any bulk shopping, because he "is a man who loves a bargain." Justine has more flexibility in her week, because she doesn't travel, so she is the family "chauffeur." However you decide to do it, make sure that the division of labor is even and, as is the case with Justine and Nick, the assigned tasks are in line with what you like to do and can do well.

Just take another peek at chapter 2 on job responsibilities and you'll be reminded about just how important it is to try to take on assignments that fit in with your skills, schedule, and interest.

Five Steps to a Highly Productive Meeting

Based on research, interviews, and our own meeting experiences, we have come up with five steps you need to take to have a highly productive meeting. While none of the action steps below should take much time, there are no shortcuts. We all waste too many hours in ineffective meetings during the day. Let's not bring *that* bad habit home.

Step One: Planning

Just as at work, a great meeting at home is the result of a little pre-planning. If this is your first meeting, then you are going to start with taking out that massive to-do list you prepared earlier in the book, a list that contained all of the jobs that needed to get done for the house and family daily, weekly, monthly, and yearly. This will be the first item that you will be reviewing together.

Second, make sure you each bring your calendar. Any social or business commitments require the family to do some juggling. It could be a work trip that takes one of you out of town and impacts how the car gets serviced, an upcoming field trip for the kids that requires buying a new sleeping bag, an upcoming birthday party that calls for finding the perfect gift, or even tickets to the theater that require a Saturday night sitter. Your children also have their own obligations that are your obligations as well. In-school events are something to consider and add to the discussion list, practices and games often require you to do the driving, while playdates and parties may mean presents as well as transportation.

You also want to make sure to bring the list of goals that

you created in chapter 1. If you have included any major goals such as retirement planning, then you will need to break that up into manageable steps (research broker, meet with accountant, set up accounts, establish budget) and add one or two of these steps to your weekly to-do list.

Last, make sure to grab the bill caddy (if you don't have one, go to a store like Staples, The Container Store, or Office Depot) and current budget so you can prioritize and plan for the bill paying. In our house we make sure that Andrew has his laptop with him during our weekly meetings so we can review our finances together and pay the bills on the spot.

Step Two: Agenda

Now that you've gathered everything for the meeting, it's time to set the agenda. Topics could include: home repairs, schedules, finances, shopping, meal planning, cleaning, paperwork, and organization.

Our agendas have looked something like this:

FRIEDMAN WEEKLY MEETING AGENDA

NOVEMBER 10

- **REVIEW LAST WEEK'S LIST**
  We recapped and updated each other on everything that was assigned the week before.

- **THANKSGIVING PLANS**
  We decided where we were going for the holiday, who needed to be called, and what we were going to bring.

- **DECEMBER CALENDAR**
  We reviewed in-school events, upcoming social plans, and business events.

- **END OF THE YEAR PLANNING**
  We discussed what appointments needed to be made and with whom and what information needed to be gathered for the accountant.

- **GOALS**
  We looked at our budget for saving for a house and took a look at the 529 college savings plan accounts.

- **BILLS AND BUDGET**
  We paid bills and reviewed current budget, setting a number for holiday gifts.

- **CHRISTMAS GIFTS**
  We started planning, beginning with names and initial thoughts for gifts.

- **MONTHLY TO-DOS**
  We looked ahead to see what we needed to fold into next week's to-do list, including car maintenance and dental appointments.

Step Three: Discussion

We are trained in the workplace to follow unspoken guidelines when participating in a meeting. There is usually a leader present who sets the tone and follows an agenda. While the rest of the attendees chime in when it makes sense for them to contribute, for the most part there is a lot of listening going on. Rarely are people vocal about their differing points of view and rarely are managers questioned on their decision making or directives. At home there are no such established guidelines, since there is no boss, so you are going to have to set your own rules.

We recommend that these meeting guidelines include:

- Active listening by both parties
- Acceptance of the other's point of view
- No arguing—instead focusing on finding solutions
- Equal listening, sharing, and directing, since there is no boss
- Taking responsibility for your own to-do list
- Bringing up-to-date calendars and lists to the meeting

Once there are guidelines, you will soon find a rhythm to your discussions. When we had our first impromptu meeting the structure was just a brainstorm on everything we had to get done and by when. We then split it into two lists—Andrew's and Caitlin's. At this point, several years later, our meetings are more focused and detailed because we are more familiar with what needs to get done. We spend more time on the big-picture planning than on the weekly chores.

Step Four: Recording

One of you will need to take notes during the weekly meeting, keeping track of those new items that were added to the list for the week as well as any next steps on projects. You don't need to be a court reporter—just create a general bullet list of what was covered. Andrew types away on his laptop during our weeklies and sends Caitlin a copy after the meeting so she can keep track of her responsibilities.

Step Five: Assigning

This is where everything you learned about job responsibilities comes into play. The key to assigning the to-dos is for each of you to leave with a list of tasks that are doable, with most falling into your comfort zone. Don't overcommit. You want to be able to get to everything on the list and not forget to do things. Before taking anything on, look at your upcoming week to gauge how much free time you actually have. For instance, Caitlin will check her week to see how many business lunches she has booked, because that will impact how many errands she can get to during the workweek. Andrew often interviews chefs at night, so he looks to see how many evenings he is going to be home to work on his list.

Once you have a better sense of your schedule, then you can take on those tasks that you can realistically get to. The list each of you ends up with should be a combination of chores you enjoy, things you are more skilled to take on, a few action items to move forward your long-term goals, improvements to your household and family, and one or two from your monthly or yearly list.

Our recent to-do lists looked like this:

Andrew
- Call the landlord about renewing the lease.
- Put together Declan's tetherball set.
- Call the landlord about the broiler.
- Buy groceries for the kids' camp lunches.
- Shop for/make risotto dish for the New Year's Eve party.
- Reorganize the basement.
- File tax paperwork.
- Go through and pay the bills (Caitlin and Andrew).

- Buy curtains for the kids' room.
- Buy dog food.

Caitlin
- Move the dinner party with George and Tansy.
- Call the insurance company about the deductible form.
- Reschedule the dentist for the kids.
- Order groceries for the week.
- Send thank-you note to woman who hosted the piano concert.
- Confirm the piano lesson for Taylor.
- Set up a playdate for Taylor and Tess.
- Go through and pay the bills (Caitlin and Andrew).
- Take Indy to the groomer.

From the Desk of . . .

As a partner in a successful branding agency with clients including Food Network and Harlequin, Adina Avery-Grossman has led thousands of meetings during her career. We asked her for tips on how to have an effective business meeting and we chimed in to remind you how these suggestions might help you with your weekly family meeting.

Same Time, Same Place

Adina tells us that if the meeting is recurring, "keep it at the same time each week (as much as you can), because it's more easily remembered and subsequently becomes a part of the rhythm of the week."

This is true for your home meeting as well. If your family has a recurring weekly meeting, then everyone knows to set aside the time for it as well as plan for it.

Get Everyone on the Same Page

Every meeting needs an agenda, including recurring items and new ones. Adina says, "An agenda will prompt participants to prepare and help manage expectations." And for those times when you get stuck on an item on the agenda, you can avoid derailing the meeting if you "just acknowledge it and put it on a flip chart. That's where you can park it for later discussion."

At home the agenda is going to be the working to-do list from the week before and any items that cropped up during the week that need to be addressed. Just as at work, without an agenda meetings lack structure and can fall apart.

Get the Right People in the Room

Adina advises us to make sure that the right people are gathered for the appropriate meeting and that, in her experience, "attendees may change/shift based on what is being discussed. While the core group might meet week to week, there may be others who could also be included."

Also true for the home meeting. While you and your partner may be meeting each week, there are certain times where what you are covering includes other people. For instance, if you have an upcoming business trip and your babysitter will be stepping in for extra child care, you might want her to join you for the meeting to review the schedule. Or, let's say your child is starting up soccer with its complicated schedule of away games and practices, then have him come to the meeting so that together you can go over the calendar.

Give People Homework

Adina insists, "It's okay to give people homework: something to think about, research, or prepare in advance of the meeting." In her experience, preparation helps make the meeting "more robust and builds engagement."

Most children come home with a backpack full of birthday party invitations, permission slips, announcements of in-school events, and other paperwork that parents are expected to review, fill out, or add to the home calendar. As your children get older, it is important that they start managing this paperwork and take ownership of keeping track of it and getting it in front of you. The weekly meeting is a good place to start building these habits. Create a place for them to put the paperwork, remind them to bring it with them to the weekly meeting, go through it together, and ask them to figure out what needs to be done with it. If there are in-school events, then add them to the family calendar and discuss who can attend. If there are birthday party invitations, then add them to the calendar during the family meeting and figure out what to get for gifts and when. All of these to-dos are opportunities to teach your kids to take responsibility for their corner of the world.

Check Cell Phones, BlackBerrys, iPhones, and iPads at the Door!

When she is conducting a meeting with her team, Adina insists that they commit to "one hour unplugged." *Reducing the distractions makes it easier to get through the agenda and focus on solving any issues.*

Ditto for the home front! Your family deserves 100 percent of your attention. Not only is it good for you to be focused on what is in front of you, but you are teaching your kids to be fully present. With kids engaging in more advanced technology at younger and younger ages, some kids have a really hard time sitting still when denied texting or gaming for more than fifteen minutes at a time. For teenagers, texting is especially distracting. Forcing them to spend one hour a week communicating only with those in the room, and without electronic devices, will foster self-reliance and self-control.

There Must Be a Leader and a NoteTaker

In Adina's experience, there should be two assigned roles for every meeting, including a leader and a notetaker. Adina tells us that "the leader should facilitate and the notetaker record, as it's very difficult to do both."

This is somewhat true for the meetings at home. One of you should have the responsibility of keeping track of what was discussed, although you will switch off who is leading the meeting based on who is going over their to-do list and follow-up from the prior week.

Leave Time for Thinking Big

Rather than spending an entire meeting on logistics and the details of running the business, Adina makes sure to leave time for bigger brainstorming when she leads meetings. "People want to feel engaged and a part of the bigger issues and the discussions of what's happening long-term. Reserve time on each agenda to encourage these discussions."

Yes! We agree that big-picture thinking is an essential part of these meetings. Not only is it empowering to tackle the bigger issues, it helps keep the small stuff in perspective and lets everyone feel like they are a part of shaping their futures. For the kids, you are offering the opportunity to practice putting things in perspective, which will come in handy later in life as they confront bigger social, academic, and emotional challenges.

Gather the Right Tools

When Adina is planning for a meeting, she makes sure that all of the right tools have been gathered and are present in the room. Adina tells us that "flip charts,

Internet access, pens, sticky notes, stapler, paper, and calendars should always be on hand. It might seem silly, but having these things in the room can enhance the discussion and help you to move things forward."

Family calendars, checkbooks, and sometimes a laptop offer you the tools to keep crossing things off the list.

No Rambling

Because meetings can easily go long if there is no control over the discussion, Adina suggests that organizers "allot time and keep to it. You'll build trust among your colleagues if you can run a one-hour meeting and have it last fifty-five minutes. It shows you are prepared and disciplined."

A shorter, more focused meeting is better for everyone. You might want to consider not only putting a time limit on the meeting but on specific topics as well. If there is a time limit, it can often push a conversation forward and force a needed resolution. If an issue isn't resolved within the allotted time, you can always bump it to another meeting and move on through the list.

Recap the Discussion

Because we've all walked out of meetings wondering if there were any next steps, Adina tells us, "Anything that is not concluded at the meeting should have next steps with timing and the responsible person attached to it. People need a reminder of what they agreed to." This absolutely applies to the home meeting as well. Everyone should leave having a list of next steps in their hands, knowing exactly what is expected of them in the following week.

In the next chapter you'll learn how to organize your workload and delegate effectively so that you won't be buried under the to-do list.

punch the clock

ORGANIZATION AND DELEGATION

Most of us have too few hours in the day, not too many. Thanks in large part to our smartphones, our workdays are spilling over into dinnertime, our kids have jam-packed schedules we manage for them, and budgets are tightening, all of which means that many of us are skipping date nights in favor of a "catch up on work" evening. With only two weeks of vacation per year for most of us, it isn't like we're going to be able to unwind at the beach anytime soon.

So when and how do we find some downtime?

We have to fight for it.

This chapter is going to turn you into an efficiency fanatic. We're going to show you how to treat your household responsibilities as a full-time job that you can only dedicate a few hours to each week. Because, let's be honest, the work is always there, even if you're doing your day job.

You are going to learn to:
- Be ruthlessly organized when tackling your to-do list.
- Prioritize everything from socializing to goal setting.
- Accept help when it's offered.
- Use the quickest (and cheapest) way to stock up on household items.
- Shave time off of every chore on your list and see where you may be wasting minutes or even hours getting things done.

We will show you how to master your list and the hours you dedicate to it, so you can rediscover that elusive downtime we all covet.

First, evaluate how much time you are spending on chores and errands and where you might be wasting time. If you run errands here and there instead of consolidating trips, you could be clocking unnecessary time and miles. When you sit in the dentist's waiting room, instead of reading an old magazine, why not take care of a few items on your list by firing off e-mails? Rather than paying bills by writing out checks, filling out envelopes, putting on stamps, and going to the post office, set up online bill paying, which takes a fraction of the time. You can find time for just about everything if you look for it.

In this chapter we'll demonstrate how tackling the hardest or least appealing job at the beginning of the week will create momentum, and how setting clear goals for each day will make the larger goals for the week feel manageable and perhaps even fun. An author and a professional organizer will share her thoughts on the big-picture benefits of clearing clutter, and a small-business owner will show us a few quick systems for sorting paperwork. We will encourage you to invest in a week-at-a-glance personal calendar to use as an integrated family planner. We'll also discuss creating a home office (or corner) for yourselves where you can establish a home "headquarters" that includes a filing system that works for all of you.

The advice in this chapter will show you how to take control of your to-do list and your schedule, thereby freeing up even more time for yourself, each other, and your family.

Cleaning House . . . Literally

Take a walk through your house. What do you see? Toys under the couches, mail piled up near the front door, unfiled paperwork stuffed in between books on the shelf, clothing that doesn't fit taking up room in your closets, and shoes the kids have outgrown still on the floor of their room? Don't feel bad if your house doesn't look the way you want it to look. Most busy working families have a high threshold for clutter. In fact, many of us don't even notice the piles until they topple over. This being said, we find it almost impossible to think clearly, make changes, or organize anything when our house is overflowing with stuff.

Before we get into how you can become more efficient, we suggest that you literally clean house. It's not just about putting things away and vacuuming the living room rug. We want you to throw out, recycle, or donate anything that doesn't work, fit, or entertain anymore. When it comes to clothing, the old adage is that if you haven't worn it in a year, donate it. If there are books you own but will never read again, give them away or drive them over to a used bookstore. Throw expired food and medicine into the garbage. Ask your kids to help out by going through their toys and games. Encourage them to donate things they don't play with anymore. Go through their closets while you are at it, and we're guessing you are going to find clothes that are now too small and belong at the Salvation Army. Are there duplicate tools and household items you have been holding on to for years that can be recycled or donated? The old television that is sitting in the basement needs to be recycled, as does the computer that died two years ago. The videocassette tapes that you hold on to for sentimental reasons, even though you don't have a VCR anymore, should be thrown out along with the scratched CDs. Pots for plants you don't have room for, rusting gardening tools, the wagon with the broken wheel, gifts that you never really liked, wires and cords that serve no purpose—all need to go.

We want you to be merciless with the stuff you don't need or have room for. This is about clearing your space so you can clear your head.

Once you have cleared out as much as you can, it's the perfect time to do a deep clean.

Now the Paperwork: Shredding, Filing, and Recycling

Let's take a closer look at the paperwork you most likely have in small (or large) piles all over the house. We are going to tell you what to save and what to toss and then how to set up a filing system that works so you are no longer drowning.

What you will need for this project:

- Shredder
- Trash can
- Recycle bin
- Pens

- Manila folders
- Hanging files and labels
- A file cabinet or a portable file holder (stores such as Staples, The Container Store, and Office Depot all have versions)
- Fireproof lockbox

Paperwork Guidelines: Filing versus Tossing
- For one month hold on to . . .
  - Receipts for minor purchases

- For one year hold on to . . .
  - Monthly retirement account statements
  - Monthly bank statements (staple to deposit/withdrawal slips)
  - Paycheck stubs (staple to deposit slips unless you have direct deposit)
  - Credit card receipts
  - Most current Social Security statement (shred the rest)

- For ten years hold on to . . .
  - Year-end statements from your bank, retirement accounts, and credit card companies
  - Receipts for major purchases (cars, computers)

- Hold on to forever . . .
  - Wills
  - Real estate paperwork, including rental agreements
  - Tax returns
  - Stock certificates and savings bonds
  - Vaccination records

In addition to the paperwork above, make sure that you put birth and death certificates, marriage licenses, Social Security cards, insurance policies, and deeds in either a safe-deposit box or a fireproof lockbox.

Now, on to the Filing

We can't overemphasize the importance of having a filing system. It is the key to wrangling the paperwork, setting yourself up for easy tax prep, and it will help you avoid any last-minute scrambling when you've been asked to verify something. Vera, a woman we interviewed for this book, told us that because she and her husband have so many bills, accounts, legal documents, activities, subscriptions, insurance plans, and tax documents, they have to have an "office-like filing system." Remember that every small home is essentially a small business. If you approach it like that and come up with systems to deal with the "business" of running a home, you will reduce your stress. You will be like

Vera who, when asked for an "immunization record, bill statement, or legal document," knows "exactly where it is."

Grab the pens, manila folders, and hanging files and let's get organized. Pull out all of the bank statements, tax paperwork, insurance policies, credit card statements, and everything else you have lying around and begin sorting. Once it has all been separated into piles, start labeling the files and folders as outlined below.

Label the Hanging Files

- Tax Returns (then label manila folders with each year you received returns going back ten years)
- Checking and Savings Accounts (manila folders for each account)
- Social Security (keep the most current statement in here)
- Mortgage/Lease
- Home (manila folder for Renovations, Warranties, Insurance)
- Investment and Retirement Accounts [manila folders for each account, including 529s, 401(k)s, SEPs (Simplified Employee Pension plans)]
- Credit Card Accounts (manila folder for each account)
- Health and Dental (policies, claims, paid bills, statements)

- Auto (manila folders for repairs, insurance, warranties)
- [Child's Name]—each child should have his or her own hanging file (manila folders for school forms, classroom policies, report cards, health records)
- Child Care (manila folders for day care and/or nanny to include receipts or copies of checks, contact information)
- Service Providers (manila folders for phone, cable, lawn care, etc.)

If you have a home office, lucky you! If not, then find a corner for this file cabinet or carrying case.

We All Need Systems

Both small and large companies have a million details being attended to by human resources, building operations, and management that most employees are unaware of, like taxes, filing, paperwork, inspections, renovations, and equipment upgrades. These things keep the company chugging along and the various systems running smoothly. We believe that by creating or adopting some of these systems at home, you can operate smoothly too. We've listed a handful of systems we suggest you try, all inspired by the office.

General Filing

We've covered the bulk of this above, but you might also consider buying an accordion file for receipts.

Family Calendar

We can't stress enough the importance of a family calendar. Some people use shared calendars through Google .com, but we prefer the old-fashioned version that we hang in our kitchen. We use the calendar to keep track of every obligation (business trip, event, birthday party, holiday, vacations, early morning meetings, etc.). To make sure it is thorough, we have a few tricks.

- As soon as the school calendar is posted online, we print it out and add all of the teacher conference days, school closings, early closings, and late mornings to the calendar.
- When the kids come home with permission slips for field trips, we add the dates to the calendar and note whether we need to pack a lunch or not.
- Birthday invitations are responded to immediately and then added to the calendar.

- If we book an appointment during the workday that is going to affect either the morning drop-off or afternoon pickup, we send ourselves an e-mail reminder to add it to the calendar.
- When we buy a new calendar, we pull out the list of birthdays and anniversaries we have compiled and add all of the dates to the calendar.

Since we use the calendar to plan gift buying, child care, days off of work, and food shopping, it has to be both up-to-date and accurate.

Mail

We actually have a system similar to the one that Holly mentioned in her interview. On a console table near the front door we have two in-boxes and a bill caddy. One in-box is labeled "To File," and the other is labeled "To Respond." The bill caddy we have is sectioned off into thirty-one days, so we drop bills into the date when it should be dropped in the mail, not when it is due. Under the console table we keep a trash can and a recycling can. Whoever comes home and gets the mail sticks bills into the caddy, invitations/letters/cards into the To Respond in-box, and the paperwork that needs to end up in the filing cabinet downstairs into the To File box. Everything else either goes into the trash can or the recycle bin.

Gifts

We went through a period of time a few years ago when there were a handful of things that perpetually fell through the cracks. One of these tasks was the birthday party gift. For some reason, we could never get to a store until an hour before the parties, which caused us all unnecessary stress. When our kids were younger, they were invited to birthday parties by almost every one of their classmates. That turned out to be about thirty parties a year. No joke. Add to that the birthdays of our friends, and family and you have a lot of presents to buy. To get this under control we began choosing a few children's gifts to buy in bulk. For the adults in our lives, whenever we came across a beautiful journal, uniquely packaged soaps, or first print runs of great books, we would buy them. Gift cards are also helpful to have on hand; consider buying a few from places like Amazon.com, iTunes, or GameStop. For us, the gift closet (really just a corner of our bedroom closet) saved us from the last-minute surprises that always had caused tension.

Travel

When you travel a lot for business, as we did, then you develop systems to make it all that much easier and fun without even realizing it. Keep prepacked a travel kit for everyone with mini-toothpastes, brushes, deodorants, and dental floss. We include Children's Tylenol, lip balm, nail clippers, a mini-sewing kit, Band-Aids, and Neosporin. Before booking our hotel rooms, we make sure the hotels we are staying in offer everything we need and double-check that amenities, like the pool, are working. The night before we leave, we print out hard copies of all of the boarding passes, hotel and car confirmations, listings of restaurants and places we want to see, and any contact information. It's also smart to photocopy your ticket and ID and put it in the top of any bags you check—that way, if they're lost, the airport has a way to get your bag back to you, and if you lose your ticket you have a copy in your suitcase.

From the Desk of . . .

Mary Carlomagno is the owner of Order, which specializes in clutter control, urban apartment solutions, office spaces, and shopping addictions. As a professional consultant and the author of Give It Up!: My Year of Learning to Live Better with Less, *and* Secrets of Simplicity, *Mary speaks to organizations such as American Express and Ameriprise about getting organized.*

We talked with Mary about what she's learned as an organizing consultant and asked her to share tips for couples struggling to create a little order at home. This is what she taught us.

Be Accountable Even at Home

So many of us are highly organized at work, but when it comes to our home we let things slide into mild or major chaos. As a professional organizer who works for clients both in and out of their offices, Mary believes that "many get more organized at work where they are being held accountable." She also believes that the key to bringing these skills into our households starts with our "being accountable to ourselves at home and eliminating procrastination." The added benefit, she says, is that "eliminating clutter is actually good for your well-being and health, so treat it like part of your maintenance routine along with exercise and a healthy diet."

The Organizing Czar

For any organizing system to work, Mary believes that "there needs to be constant updating of the family calendar, chalkboard, or whatever device the couple chooses, so that communication remains the touchstone." She recommends empowering the "person that is more organized than the other" with the device.

Coming Up for Air

Mary has advice for anybody buried in old bank statements, paid bills, and receipts; it starts with "maintenance and storage." She recommends "the ABC method: (A) things that need to be close by stay on the top of the desk; (B) things that need to be easily reachable go in a desk drawer; (C) things that are archival go somewhere like the top of the closet." Most of us tend to keep outdated paperwork around rather than putting it away somewhere. Mary suggests "taking a simple test with an item to see where it fits in the ABC system and then find a place for it." And don't forget to buy yourself a fire-safe box for the really important paperwork such as deeds, wills, and life insurance plans.

The Art of Delegation

Many of you have spent the last several years at your job developing management skills to get the best work out of your employees, to inspire loyalty, and to make the company run better, but at home you avoid reminding the babysitter not to leave her dirty dishes on the table, because you don't want to burden her. Even those of us who don't manage employees know that sometimes people just need to be told what to do, yet we don't do it with the people in our home. Babysitter, parent, friend: We don't redirect whoever it is that is helping us at home, even if something is being done incorrectly. *Stop!* The babysitter is there to make your life easier, not harder; most important, the babysitter works for you. Sure, in the short term it's easier to complain about everything you have to do at home than to have a discussion with someone else that may or may not be uncomfortable, but if you take this path of avoidance, it will never get better for you. There is only one of you and a limit to how much you can do and how much time you have to do it. If you don't start delegating, then your to-do list won't ever get smaller. This section will serve as a reminder that all of those great delegation skills you employ at work every day *do* have a place in your personal life, too. And we aren't just going to teach you to delegate to the people you pay to help you; we want you to look at your partner, your children, and even your in-laws as potential helpers. But get ready to learn or relearn how to delegate, because there is an art to getting the people around you to want to help you and to do tasks the way you want them done.

What Is Delegation?

In the most basic sense, delegation is giving someone work to do—and often it's the work that was originally on your list and you have now put it on someone else's. If you are a supervisor at work, you are likely responsible for your department and the work of your direct reports. *But* you don't do everything, do you? They have their lists and you have your list. Bring that thinking home and suddenly you will see that there are people in your life who could actually help you.

Why Delegate?

Primarily, delegating makes your life easier and more fun by freeing up some of the time you are spending working at home. When delegation is done respectfully, it can also help you strengthen the relationships you have with your partner and employees. Think how your partner would feel if, due to an increase in your business travel, you hand over an important project like your child's birthday party and you express your utter trust and faith in his ability to get it done. Then, encourage him during the process—don't question his decisions—and applaud the results. Not only have you freed up the time you need to focus on your job by giving the party planning away, but your partner feels trusted and supported by you. We say this is a win-win.

Businesses Today

Unlike ten or even five years ago, managers are trained now to delegate horizontally instead of the more common delegate-down process. The team approach has shown to improve efficiency and communication throughout departments. So at home the skills you need to delegate effectively will be the same whether you are leaving the design of your garden to your landscaper or your partner is taking on researching the perfect place to live. Remember, delegating is not dumping your work on someone else. Delegating is giving someone responsibility and decision-making authority for a project or task. There also needs to be accountability when someone takes on a task. It is now, in every sense, "their job." In addition, if you are feeling as if you "always" do something around the house, delegate it!

People You Can Delegate To

- Your partner
- The kids
- Your parents or in-laws if they are close by or when they visit
- Your employees (everyone, that is, on your household payroll)

Why Don't You Delegate More at Home?

Here are some of the reasons people we interviewed gave us for not delegating and what we think about their reasons.

"It takes forever to explain how to use the online bill paying."

It may take forever to explain how to do anything the first time, but once you take the time to train your partner, mother-in-law, daughter, or sitter how to do something around the house, you're done.

"I like the vacuuming done a certain way."

You can actually show someone how you want something done. If he doesn't follow your directions, then retrain him. Consider giving him a reason for why you have a preference for how it gets done; it will be easier for him to remember when there is a reason attached.

"I can put away the clothes faster."

You most likely can do it faster, but so what? If you are doing more than your share, then how much time are you really saving at the end of the day? Wouldn't it be better to let go of some of your list to free up some of your time?

"I am better at making dinner for the kids."

Anyone can get better at something if she puts in the effort, so give your family, employees, or friends the chance to help you and improve their skills.

Signs That You Are Not Delegating Enough

- You feel like you are doing everything.
- You are stressed out and angry . . . a lot.
- You aren't able to get through your list. Ever.
- Your employees have huge chunks of time where they are doing nothing.

What to Delegate

Pull out the weekly to-do list, as well as the short-term and long-term goals, and see what you can thoughtfully pass along. Consider your partner a resource when you need the support, think about how you can utilize the time that you are already paying someone for, and discuss the opportunities for your children to jump in and help out.

STEPS FOR EFFECTIVE DELEGATION

1. Choose the tasks that you are going to delegate.
2. Really think about the right person to do the task.
3. Take the time to explain the task and make sure that you have supplied him with all of the tools, equipment, and information he needs to do the job.
4. Be available the first time he does the task so you can answer questions or help him if he needs it.
5. Give positive feedback and show your appreciation.
6. If you are open to it, solicit his suggestion for how to do the task better or more efficiently. That way, he will start to "own" the job.
7. Accept that people aren't exactly like you and will approach tasks differently than you would. Let them.

Remember, if you delegate well, then you will end up with more support, more time, and a group of people who want to help you.

Ideas for Getting Efficient

Your home is clean, your paperwork is filed away, and you are ready to learn how to become superefficient. A note about efficiency: Being efficient does not mean being sloppy and doesn't mean that you rush through projects because you can. It means that you take a few moments to think things through before acting. Rather than jumping into the car to do one errand on Saturday morning, you step back and think about what else you have on your list for the week and maybe add a few more stops. Instead of just buying groceries for the week ahead, you look into adding bulk items to the list so you can have them on hand for the month. Being efficient is taking a few minutes to think about doing things better, smarter, faster with an end goal of having more personal time each week.

Maximize the Internet

We all know how much commerce is being done on the Web these days, especially around the holidays. But we now use the Internet for all sorts of things: online banking; ordering our groceries, prescriptions, clothing, and back-to-school supplies; making travel reservations; signing the kids up for camp; and even buying pet food. One of the many benefits to taking care of business online is that you can do it during a lunch break, while watching TV, or while commuting to the office (if you take a bus or a train or someone else is doing the driving). Most online retailers will alert you to sales, so you can often save money as well.

Stock Up

Keeping a well-stocked house—everything from paper goods to toiletries to greeting cards and wrapping paper—reduces trips to stores. We've told you about our gift closet, but we also have boxes of cards for every occasion, wrapping paper, and extras of the items we often run out of—like laundry detergent and shampoo. You don't need to stock up your house like a general store, but having extras of a few things on hand can save you from the last-minute errand.

One Calendar

Keeping a consolidated schedule of plans so you can check each other's availability and commitments without having to call or e-mail each other repeatedly during the business day will help you save time.

Organization Is Key

Have systems that don't require face-to-face communication, such as a bill caddy for the person whose job it is to pay bills, a receipts box for the person who keeps the checkbook, a shopping list on the fridge, and so on.

Consolidate Errands

Map out errands to avoid driving or walking in circles to get things crossed off the list.

Fit It In

You don't need to spend all Saturday morning doing errands. Fit in a few on the way to work, during lunchtime, and on the way home. Doing this might save you hours for fun stuff on the weekend.

Use Waiting Time

Even fifteen minutes of free time can be valuable. While waiting at the dentist's office make a list of people you want to socialize with, schedule an appointment while in line at the bank, and so on.

Ten Essential Items for Organization

1. Bill caddy
2. File hangers and folders

3. Accordion files (receipts)

4. Family calendar

5. Dry-erase board for the kitchen

6. In-boxes

7. Shredder

8. Storage containers

9. Shelving (we have shelves everywhere)

10. Box of office supplies (pens, staplers, labels)

True Story: Working Together, Playing Together

Jacqueline and Cameron Wilson are the cofounders and principal conservators behind Wilson Conservation. Launching their business together in 1998, after two years of unofficially working together, Jacqueline and Cameron are considered the best in the business and are hired to help restore both private and public sculpture collections all over the world. We spoke to them about how they manage to run a business together while juggling parenthood and a marriage with what looks like minimal drama. We interviewed them about how they keep balance, raise their daughter, split up jobs, and still, at the end of the day, find time for each other.

We Are in This Together

Jacqueline and Cameron have the same challenges that many of us have, plus they juggle a business together. The "biggest challenge is satisfying the demanding needs and deadlines of our clients and being available as parents and playmates with our seven-year-old daughter, Tess." Unfortunately, like most of us, their needs "as a couple are last to be served; carving out time for us has not been successful."

We must make time for each other; otherwise, it is all just work. Commit to at least a few hours each week when you aren't focused on getting things done but rather enjoying the other person.

Translatable Skills

The advantage that they have at running a business and a home together is that Jacqueline and Cameron know their strengths and weaknesses when it comes to getting things done. At work Cameron "often meets with clients and does the majority of traveling for business." Jacqueline has found that her strength lies in her "ability to multitask and manage numerous projects at once." They feel that their business strengths "are carried out in [their] home life." Jacqueline takes care of "taxes and managing the house-hold funds," just like their office. Cameron takes care of "minor repairs and the garden," which is in line with the hands-on work he does for the clients and their business. At the office Jacqueline manages the scheduling and at home she oversees the family calendar. They share care of their daughter, Tess.

If you don't work together or own a business together, find out what each of you is good at in the workplace. It is those skills—organization, leadership, creativity, focus—that, when applied to the right task at home, will help things run more efficiently.

Bumps at Home and Bumps at Work

As we mentioned at the beginning of the book, we met and fell in love while working at a public relations busi-ness. Some of the personality conflicts we had at the office occasionally crop up at home twelve years later. Caitlin is still terrible with details and tends to forget plans; Andrew is still a bit of a micromanager. In the Wilsons' case, they have conflicts at home and at work about their individual capacity for work. Jacqueline manages the details at work, keeping a close eye on the to-do list, because she likes to get things done. At home, she is just as task-oriented, oftentimes cleaning or organizing when they have a little downtime, which she admits "does not make for a relaxing weekend." She said she "gets satisfaction from accomplishing things." But since Cameron wants to use the downtime to read the paper, not cross things off the list, "it's a source of dissension and an area where we struggle as a partnership and a couple."

Accept how the other person works. Your partner may very well have a completely different skill set and approach to her to-do list. Let her do it in her time and in her way, but that means that both of you must honor your commitments and promises. If you say you are going to do the laundry, then you have the right to do it your way, but do it. It will reduce the tension and conflict if neither party feels micromanaged.

A Good Team

Cameron's "affability" and Jacqueline's "ability to multitask and organize" serve their business and clients well. They have a shared philosophy about "money and work ethics" and are both eager to please their clients. They would rather "lose money and make a client happy than make money and deliver an inferior product." This shared commitment to quality and customer service has allowed the business seamlessly to become an extension of their personal lives. They are "very social and enjoy the deep friendships" that they have cultivated in their professional life.

Shared values help you build a strong foundation and network in both your personal and professional lives. It is important to recognize and reflect the priorities of your partner at home. If it's important to your partner to eat dinner together every night as a family, then make sure that becomes part of your weekly plan.

Time to Draw Lines

Since they run the business together and out of their home, it is an ongoing challenge to separate their personal lives from their professional lives. It's harder for Jacqueline to draw the line because, by her own admission, she is a "workaholic and perfectionist." According to Jacqueline, "Cameron can come home and forget it all." She struggles with "shutting it off and being fully present" at home.

If your partner has a hard time being present and is often too wrapped up in what needs to get done, then help her by spending a set amount of time each day reviewing the list together. The five minutes you take going over what needs to be accomplished that day or that week might be all your partner needs to let it go for a little while.

. . .

We hope that the advice in this chapter will help you get organized and clutter-free (or at least clutter-reduced). In the following chapter we are going to cover how to make the most of the help that is available to you from family and friends or an employee.

the home team

EMPLOYEE RELATIONS

Consider this: The babysitter you hire for Saturday nights, the accountant who sifts through your receipts each tax season, even the teenager who mows your front lawn are all to some degree your *employees*. It's amazing how many people we pay without ever thinking of them that way. Even with a handful of hourly employees reporting to you, most of you don't spend even a second considering how you might be better managers at home. If you did, you might receive a higher level of work and have better communication with the people who come in and out of your houses and your lives. We all learn the hard way that unless you treat the hiring, managing, or firing of your personal employees in the same professional manner you do at work, you are throwing money away and creating the potential for awkward situations down the line.

This chapter will show you how to put on your manager's hat. We'll walk you through how to create clear expectations for everyone from a dog walker to a housepainter, how to delegate respectfully without micromanaging, and how to get the best work from someone you hire. You'll also find interview questions to ask potential employees, plus tips for hiring and firing someone.

The section "Yes, Even the Babysitter" will offer interview questions created to find and retain the best candidate for any job related to your home. Later in this chapter, an accountant and a lawyer will weigh in on the legal and financial ramifications of having an employee at home (e.g., taxes, Social Security, insurance) and the value of checking references.

This chapter includes advice on how and why to write an "employee manual" (usually just one sheet of dos and don'ts) for anyone working within your home and tips on how to figure out whom you hire and what kind of job they are doing. An interview with a human resources executive includes suggestions for finding, interviewing, and keeping the ideal candidate. A list of inexpensive hourly employees offers solutions that can make enormous differences in the home without breaking the budget.

Managing is hard for most of us in the office. It's even harder at home when we are trying to relax, drop our public/professional masks and scripts, and just be ourselves.

To address the challenges that we all have being the boss, this chapter will offer advice for rewarding, redirecting, and confronting your employees. You will also find specific tips and ideas about how to improve your relationship with your employees, how to save money when it comes to negotiating salaries, and how to keep the emotion from exacerbating any uncomfortable discussion.

Who Are Your Employees and How Are They Doing?

When you take on a new management position, it is likely that you are also taking on employees that you haven't worked with before. This new team you have in front of you is either going to help you achieve what you were hired to do or not. If, after a few weeks, you see that an employee is actually a roadblock to getting your job done, you will most likely fire him. If your employee could be an asset to your team with a little redirection and training, then you most likely will keep him on. If your employee is an asset already, then you will most likely figure out how to keep him happy.

We want the two of you to think of yourselves as a pair of new managers hired to run your home. We want you to look at the people who help you with child care, cleaning, health care, or your financial well-being as your employees. For you to do a good job running your household, these people on your personal payroll need to be hardworking, well-trained employees, and the right fit.

So we ask you to take a look at whom you have working for you, spend time evaluating their contribution, and consider how much you are paying them. You might realize at the end of this exercise that you need to make some changes, spend more time training the people who work in your house, or make more of an effort to reward them because they are just that great.

Step One

Take out a piece of paper (and your bank statements if you need a reminder) and write down every single person you have paid to do a personal service for your household.

Your list may include:

- Babysitter
- Gardener/lawn mower/landscaper
- Pediatrician
- General practitioner
- Medical specialist
- Accountant/bookkeeper
- General contractor/carpenter/housepainter
- Specialty teacher (piano teacher/math tutor/ballet teacher)
- Financial adviser

- Dog walker
- Veterinarian
- Auto repair specialist
- House cleaner

Step Two

Next to the names, make a few notes about the services these employees provide for you.

Step Three

Figure out how much you pay these people. If you only hire them a few times a year, make a note of the total you spend on this employee. If it's babysitters and you pay them weekly, then make a note of that.

Step Four

Consider the services these employees are providing and how much you pay them. Are you getting your money's worth? Do these employees add to the quality of your household? Do they do a good job or a bad job and why?

Step Five

Based on everything you have going on in your home and your to-do list, is there something else that these employees could be doing for you? Or is there a service that you don't need anymore? In other words, are the job descriptions current?

Your Best Team: Consider the Options

Although you might be uncomfortable looking at the people who work on and in your house as employees, they are. And if they are employees, then it is up to you to define their jobs and set the standards for how you want the jobs done. It's too often the case that while we have limited patience at the office for low-quality work, at home we often bend over backward for employees who are letting us down. A little objectivity is not such a bad thing at home. So take a deep breath and accept that you deserve the best work that someone can give you, from renovating your kitchen to tutoring your child. When considering all of the information you wrote down during the previous exercise, let's consider the next steps you'll want to take with each of your employees. Remember that the goal of all of this is to set up a support system that is actually supporting you, your family, and your home.

Maintain the Status Quo

Your employees are doing a good job and you don't need to change their job description. This could be the teenagers who come over twice a month to mow the lawn—you don't need them to do any more, they do a good job, and they aren't asking for a raise. If they are exceptional employees, you may want to consider demonstrating your appreciation for their great work. It doesn't have to be raise or a bonus. There are many ways to show employees that you value them, starting with telling them. At work, Caitlin makes it a point to send her team the occasional note about how much she respects their contribution. She also makes sure to acknowledge birthdays and holidays with gifts. If your employees spend the bulk of their day in your home, then make a point to stock the foods and drinks they like. Buy them their own mug to keep at your house, along with their favorite type of tea of coffee. The point is to show them in as many ways as possible that they are a valuable addition to your household.

Update Job Descriptions

Your needs have changed and you have employees who you feel can meet your needs with some adjustment to their job descriptions. For instance, your child is heading into kindergarten, so your babysitter will be free for the bulk of the day. You like this babysitter and want her to stay with your family, so instead of watching your child during the day, you would like her to shift over into more housekeeping-type work before heading over to the school for pickup. This may or may not appeal to your babysitter, but she is a valuable part of your household and can still be a strong support if the job changes a bit based on your new needs. In this case, we would recommend laying out the new job description and presenting it to the employee.

Redirect

At the office, if you found yourself with a great employee who wasn't communicating in the most efficient way possible, you would coach him on how to address this. This is redirecting an employee. You may find yourself doing the same with your home-based employees if you like their work but they aren't quite doing it in the way you would like them to do it. Our daughter had a piano teacher once who kept coming slightly early. This doesn't seem like the biggest deal, except in our case we were already running to pick up Taylor at school and then rushing to get back in time to meet the piano teacher, often making it with only five minutes to spare. Coming early in our case meant that he was standing on our steps waiting for us, causing unnecessary stress. In this case, we just told him what our situation was and moved our daughter's class time so he could fit in another student and we could have more time to get home.

Mary Riley, a management consultant we interviewed, suggests that if you are having an issue with an employee, "just pull her aside and, by using specific detailed examples, tell her what you've noticed." If the employee's behavior or attitude has changed, then try to find out what is going on. Is the job no longer a good fit, is it a personal situation that is impacting her work, or does she just need more communication from you? You want to offer specific examples of how you would like things to improve, how you will help her, and what support you can give. If tardiness is an issue, then make sure she understands how this impacts you and your family. If she isn't talking to your kids in a way that you are comfortable with, then be direct about the words and tone you don't want to hear used in your home. Real-life, specific examples always help people to improve the quality of their work. We have to make a note here about approaching these discussions as drama-free as possible. If you are obviously angry or frustrated, then the employee might not be able to get past your emotions to hear what you are telling her. As is true at work, if you are too upset to deliver the information in a nonvolatile way, pick a calmer time to raise the issue.

Downsize

You have reviewed the services provided by an employee and what you pay her and you realize that you need to downsize. When our children were born, we knew how important it was for us to have our own time, and we had a standing arrangement with a babysitter for every Saturday night. This lasted six years, until we realized a few things: Our babysitter's rates were going up every year, so she was now really expensive, and some Saturdays we didn't feel like going out but were committed to the time. So we had to let her go from the weekly sitting and went back to freelance—hiring her for the occasional job.

Human Resources 101

Again, at home you have no human resources department to search for and vet employees on your behalf, but we can still learn from the experts in HR about the process of finding and hiring the best employee. We've included below the process as outlined for us by a friend in the HR industry. The steps and thinking that go into a corporate hire are ones you should take back home.

Identify Your Needs

In the office if you are requesting a new hire, you are asked to start with a job description that outlines the needs you want an employee to fulfill. We highly recommend that you make yourself create this list for your personal employees as well. Writing a job description will force you to think through exactly what you need help with and the scope of the job. If you have it done before you interview someone, then you will know exactly how to position the job for the candidates. Thinking through your needs also makes it easier to come to a decision about whom to hire, because it will be less about liking the person and more about how well that person can do the job—just as at work.

So what are the various kinds of needs? There are short-term needs for one-off projects like cleaning the garage or painting the house. There are long-term needs that usually require a commitment of a year or more, such as home care for an elderly relative, child care for your preschooler, or a total gut renovation of the house.

These job descriptions are going to be very different: A strong teenager with eight hours free each week could take care of the garage project, but you will need to go a little wider and deeper to find a health care professional to take on the home care position. Finding the right person starts with figuring out what you need.

Write a Job Description

It's important for you to write up a job description. This will make it easier to explain to prospective candidates what you are looking for and will enable you to present the job clearly during the interview process. You have done the work to think through what needs you are trying to fulfill. Now draft it out as a one-page document. For reference, look at a few job listings online. You will see that you start with what the job is, what skills are needed to meet the responsibilities, the hours, the pay, and the qualifications.

Set the Details and the Benefits

For part-time or full-time employees, such as an in-home child care provider, it is worth thinking about the following before you start meeting with people: How much vacation time are you willing to give? Which holidays will they have off? Are you going to give them an annual bonus? When we interviewed our accountant, Nancy Adams, about this, she recommended that you look into your state's labor laws when thinking about your policies. She tells us that the law may require that you give your employees "written notice about your policies on sick leave, vacation, personal leave, holidays, and working hours."

Figure Out a Budget

How much you have to spend on getting help is the next big question and one that can't be answered until you take a look at your personal financial picture, which includes how much you have on hand and bring in monthly against how much you spend and the cost of your long-term goals and responsibilities (e.g., buying a house, paying for college). You also have to weigh this all against how much time you have to spend doing the job yourself. We have often spent a little more money than we should have getting an extra pair of hands because we were on deadlines and just couldn't find the time to do everything. But be realistic when you set a budget by asking around or researching online the average pay for the job. Make sure you speak to your accountant to get a big-picture look at the financial ramifications of hiring someone. There is often more to paying an employee than just the weekly salary; you need to consider taxes, disability, and other costs associated with having an employee.

Find Candidates

Because you most likely won't be taking out a want ad or posting the job on Monster.com, your main resource is your network and community. If you are looking for a babysitter, then ask all of your friends, the parents of your kids' friends, your kids' teachers, and your neighbors. If you are looking for a housepainter, then ask the local hardware store for their recommendations, and ask them for the name of a handyman while you're at it. There might be a blog for your town, or your school community could have a Google group up—post your needs there. The point is that once you know what you need, then start talking to everyone you can.

Interview Candidates

We've included an interview with a babysitter in this chapter to encourage you to treat this process as seriously as you do at the office. The person you hire will be in your home and around your children and possessions. You need someone who is not only capable of doing the job, but is trustworthy, reliable, and friendly. Don't be afraid to ask tough questions. Lisa Pozarowski, a director of human resources, suggests starting with asking prospective candidates what they know about the position. Then she says to "explain the job in great detail and then ask them again if they are interested in taking it." If you ask them why they think they are the right fit, then you can make sure that they aren't just desperate for work. Lisa also offered that depending on what the job is, your entire family might benefit from having a round of interviews with the candidate. "You, your partner, and your children should all be in the process."

Great Interview Questions We've Encountered

1. What would your best friend tell me about your strengths and weaknesses?
2. Tell me about a time in a previous job where you did not agree with your boss. How did you handle it?
3. Give me an example of a time when you had to make a quick decision. What problems did you face and what was the result?
4. Tell me about a change that happened at work that was very challenging. How did you handle it and what did you learn?
5. Describe a time when you had a conflict with someone, either at work or at school.
6. Describe a time when your previous boss gave you feedback. What was your reaction?
7. Describe a situation where a coworker, classmate, or friend was doing something dishonest. How did you handle it?
8. What kinds of things put you under pressure?
9. How do you manage doing multiple things at once?
10. Tell me a time when you disagreed with a rule and what you did about it.

Check References

It is essential to check references for anyone you are considering bringing into your home . . . for anything. Your office wouldn't think of hiring someone without making a few calls to their previous employers first, and neither should you. Your potential employee has a work history that you should know about. Lisa Pozarowski advises us to check both "personal and professional" references to get a better sense of the employee. Most companies do official background checks, but you can do this yourself by using social media sources. When Caitlin ran her public relations business, she would check out the candidate's pages on both Facebook and LinkedIn. Again, we tend to want to take off our professional hat when we walk in the front door, but when you are in a hiring process, it is definitely not the time to do it. Also make sure that your potential employee is legally allowed to work in the United States. You don't want to get caught hiring someone without a green card. As for the actual calls with potential references, you want to create a friendly tone because you want the former employer to feel comfortable sharing with you. Make sure to find out why the employee is no longer with the former employer. Your candidate's view on this could be very different from the former employer's. Lisa Pozarowski doesn't offer any specific questions to ask the reference, but she encourages us to try to get a clear "understanding of the candidate's job performance and areas where the former employer thinks the candidate is strong or weak."

Draft an Offer Letter

For an employee such as a nanny, you may want to consider drafting up an offer letter, which would include the job description, the pay, and the benefits. Lisa Pozarowski suggests creating an offer letter that is also the work agreement both parties sign.

Train Your Employees

Set your employees up for success by giving them all of the tools and information they need to do the job well. This includes communicating your expectations so they know what you are looking for from them. If you have a nanny starting to work with you, then plan to spend the first few mornings with her or, better yet, a whole day, so you can demonstrate how you want the meals made, the laundry done, the playdates set up, and the park visit to go. If you are hiring a neighborhood kid to help you set up and run a tag sale, tell him exactly how you want things put out, how you want potential buyers approached, if you are willing to negotiate, where you want the money kept. Sometimes training can be a five-minute conversation but, just as in the office, you can't expect a new employee to read your mind. Lisa Pozarowski suggests taking time at the start of the first day to review the details about "how he will get paid, time off, the review process, punctuality, attendance, and sick days."

Fire When Necessary

You have an employee who straight up isn't doing her job well. Unfortunately, at home there is no human resources department and, just like the hiring, the firing is on you. Firing someone is never easy. We all have bills to pay and many of us have families to support. But unlike at work, where the salary of the bad employee is affecting the company's bottom line, at home you are spending your post-tax dollars on someone. If the employee is doing something egregious, like stealing from you, then show her the door immediately. If the employee just isn't up to par, she is constantly late, or she has shown herself to be a little lazy, then you should give her a few clear warnings before you let her go; you are giving her the opportunity to turn it around.

We've had terrible experiences with bad employees,

mostly because neither of us wants to be the bad guy and outright fire them. We once had a carpenter who was working on renovating our porch. Not only would he often miss entire days on the job, but he also forgot to order the rights parts for a window, leaving a gaping hole in the side of our house for weeks. Rather than confronting him on the missteps, we let each incident pass, until one day he just stopped showing up. We learned later that he had been arrested. We also had a nanny once whom we just never really clicked with. She was fine with the kids, slightly unenergetic, but we had been given such a rave recommendation that we thought it was us. Eventually she proved to be uncomfortably disengaged, not calling to check in after our son (her charge) had surgery, and so we let her go. A day or two later we were pulled aside by another mother in our building who told us that she had often seen this nanny sitting in our lobby on her phone while our children were strapped for *hours* in their stroller.

The point of these stories is that you need to protect your family and your house. That is your number one priority. Sharing constant feedback helps you and your employee stay on the same page and gives the employee the opportunity to improve. If you are getting a feeling that something is off with someone working for you, chances are you are right. Let him go early in the relationship if it isn't working out for you. Don't put off an uncomfortable conversation; it will just get increasingly more uncomfortable the longer he is with you.

When you do fire someone, have specific examples in hand to explain why it isn't working. Think through ahead of time if you want to offer this person any type of severance. This decision should be based on why you are firing the person, how long she has worked for you, what kind of wiggle room you have in your budget, and doing "the right thing" by this person you are letting go. In the case of the neglectful nanny, we gave her two weeks because at that point all we knew was that we didn't like her style. Obviously, we didn't give the carpenter a severance because we never saw him again. Lastly, treat the person you are firing with respect, and be direct and clear with her about why it's happening, but don't offer to do anything you won't follow through on (e.g., don't promise to provide a reference).

From the Desk of . . .

We have worked with Nancy Adams for years as both our personal and corporate accountant. She has guided us through big things (starting a business together) and small things (faxing in the right paper-work to the state). She is a straight shooter with solid advice, and we knew she could give us tips we could pass on to you for covering yourself financially when you hire an in-home employee.

Financial Ramifications Beyond the Weekly Check

Nancy tells us that you need to check in with an accountant before you hire anyone. The accountant will look into any state laws that may impact you. In New York State you must pay your employee at least the minimum wage and "you must pay overtime at one and a half times your employee's basic rate after forty hours of work in a calendar week." And Nancy reminds us that a full-time employee working in your home must get at least one day off per week.

As for financial ramifications, "You will be obligated to match employee FICA and Medicare contributions, and also to pay federal taxes," and you may have to cover state unemployment taxes. Nancy warns that "if you do not plan properly, those taxes can be a surprise."

In addition, "the federal government wants you to adjust your withholdings or make quarterly payments to address the 'Nanny Tax,' which is reported in your regular federal income tax return. They may assess a penalty if you have a large balance due with your return as a result of this additional tax." Your accountant will look into state tax laws that may require you to file a "quarterly combined payroll unemployment and withholding form and pay as you go." Yes, for most of us this tax stuff is overwhelming and slightly intimidating. Don't worry, your accountant knows this like the back of her hand . . . just ask her to walk you through the tax laws as they pertain to employees.

Local/State/Federal Paperwork

Nancy tells us, "You must obtain a Federal Employer Identification Number (FEIN), which can be obtained online at the www.irs.gov website." Depending on your state, you may have to take the FEIN and register with the state as an employer to get the Employer's Registration number (ER).

You also will need to speak to your insurance broker because, Nancy tells us, "if your employee works forty hours per week, you are obligated to carry worker's compensation and short-term disability insurance."

Off the Books?

Not surprisingly, Nancy warns against paying a full-time employee off the books, which could have significant implications for you if you were caught. Just think about the politicians in recent history who were disqualified from running for public office for failing to comply with the rules. She warns us that if it were to come to the attention of the authorities, you would "owe the back payroll taxes, as well as fines for late payment of the taxes" and "if your full-time employee were injured, you could be personally responsible for their medical bills." If you decide to pay someone off the books, you are also impacting your own tax situation because you wouldn't be able to take a child care credit for these expenses. And let's not forget what Nancy refers to as the "human level"; not reporting their Social Security earnings "prevents them from accumulating a basic benefit for their future."

Yes, Even the Babysitter

The main point of this chapter is that you should hire and manage someone at home the way you do at the office. To end up with the best person for the job at a price you can afford, you need to ask the tough questions up front, check references, and be honest about your expectations.

If you treat the hiring process professionally at the beginning, it will reduce the possibility of misunderstandings down the road, because both you and the employee will know what to expect from the relationship. The interview is your chance to establish ground rules and boundaries, so treat the candidate as you would any potential new hire at the office, maintaining a friendly but professional distance. (We all want to be liked, but getting too casual with an at-home employee can make it difficult to course-correct if problems arise.) Remember, just as at the office, this person is not your friend; she is, or soon will be, an employee.

To illustrate this point, we offer you interview questions for a potential babysitter. While it may seem odd to prepare interview questions for a fourteen-year-old, make no mistake—this is a valuable employee with a lot of responsibility. Just because you are desperate to hire someone so you can get out on Saturday night doesn't mean you should overlook references or skip important information, such as her hourly rate, in an interview.

Interview Questions for a Babysitter

1. What's your experience?

   This is an obvious question but one that might get forgotten when you are in a pinch. If the babysitter has no experience with an infant and your child is an infant, then she might not be the best fit. Infant care is very different from what's required for a five-year-old.

2. How late can you work?

   If the babysitter is in high school, then it's likely he has a curfew, especially on weeknights. Best to know this before you hire him to cover a late-night engagement.

3. What do you do with kids before bedtime?

   If you don't want her sticking the kids in front of the television, then ask her about specific games or art projects she has done in the past to keep her charges busy. This question will also help you gauge her level of enthusiasm and engagement. We've had sitters who jump right into playing with the kids and others who would rather text their friends. Since you are paying the same for both employees, wouldn't it be better to hire the one who is devoted to doing a good job?

4. Do you have references?

Even if it's your neighbor's daughter, you want to know what she is like as an employee, so call those references. You might want to find out the following:

- Has the sitter ever been late? If so, how often and under what circumstances?
- Give me an example of the sitter demonstrating responsibility while with your kids.
- Has the sitter ever canceled? If so, with how much notice and for what reason?
- Tell me how the sitter spent time with your kids.
- Did the sitter follow your instructions regarding bedtime, snacks, television, and cleaning up?

5. How much do you charge an hour?

You should have a number in mind, but it's worth asking how much he's looking for. Just as in a company, if there is a big difference between what you want to pay and what he wants to charge, it's better to get it out in the open.

6. What are your transportation needs?

You can't assume anything these days, so make sure that your role in her transportation is worked out ahead of time. If she is too young to drive, will her parents drop her off or pick her up? If you live in a city, does she expect cab fare? Does she expect you to drive her home? Make sure you ask her where she lives. If it's twenty minutes away, you aren't going to want to spend forty minutes getting her home after a late night.

7. Do you have a cancellation policy?

Sounds crazy, but think about it. Just like a freelancer sets aside time for a project, the babysitter has set aside hours of billable time for you. If you are the one canceling at the last minute, he might expect a partial or complete payment. You should set and live by a policy up front.

The Employee Handbook

On your first day at a new job, you are usually given an orientation and an employee handbook. This handbook often includes a snapshot of the company itself, rules and regulations, a holiday schedule, and a copy of your offer letter. You most likely read it only when you have a question about your insurance coverage or the sick day policy, but you will review it at some point. At home it's a good idea to provide employees with similar information, although to varying degrees of detail depending on the job they have with you. Obviously, the full-time nanny is going to need more information about how the house runs, in addition to her specific job, than the handyman helping you install a cabinet.

Here is the information that most companies include in their employee handbooks. You may want to include additional information, such as a copy of the offer letter.

- Compensation information (wage, taxes, worker's compensation, when they will get paid, how they will get paid, will they get overtime)
- Work schedule (attendance, punctuality and reporting sick days, breaks, meals)

- Standards of conduct (dress code, personal calls, meals)
- Safety and security (emergency numbers, use of keys/locks and alarms)
- Computers and media (policies about use of television, computers, and phones)
- Benefits
- Leave policies (policies on vacation, holiday, sick days, and bereavement)
- Performance (policies regarding situations that would lead to immediate termination and behavior that will result in warnings)
- Reviews (when do they happen and how performance will be judged)
- Smoking (policies)

For Everyone Who Works in Your Home

You might want to consider having a binder that includes the following information for guests and employees to access. It's a guide to how your home runs and what to do in an emergency. We created a one-sheet with a lot of this information on there and posted it on our fridge so that any of the babysitters we hired could easily access it. Having all of this information available also reduces the emergency phone calls.

Emergency Phone Numbers

- Employer's cell phones
- Fire Department
- Poison Control
- Local police station
- Family doctor/pediatrician
- Veterinarian and local animal hospital
- Local hospital

Additional Household Contacts

- Neighbors
- Plumber
- Electrician

Transportation

- Local taxi phone number
- Bus or subway maps

Instructions for Television Trash and Recycling System Appliances

- Any policies about using certain appliances and any specifics about how they run

For the babysitter, all of the above plus . . .

- Allergies (any allergies that your children have should be noted along with what to do in an emergency, such as an asthma attack)

- Snacks (policies on what and when)
- Meals (policies on what and when)
- Medication (policies on use of and specific approved medications)
- Bath (which bathroom and when)
- Bedtimes (when)
- Television (how much, what, and when)
- Homework (policies on when to get it done and for how long they should be working on it)

Ten Ways to Be a Better Manager . . . at Home

1. Be Clear

We are talking specifically about being clear about what you want your employee to do and how you want it done. Begin by outlining your expectations during the interview process and sustain those expectations once you have someone on board.

2. Show Appreciation

Everyone thrives when they feel appreciated for the work they do. Think about your office: A pat on the back from a colleague feels good and a note from your boss feels even better. To motivate your in-home employees, demonstrate your appreciation for their hard work.

3. Listen

Just as the direct report needs your support or input on projects at the office, your household employees may need directions and encouragement in the same way. Maybe your nanny could use confirmation that she is doing a good job with mealtime for the kids or she would love to share a playground story with you. It's important to make yourself available to her for a personal connection at least a few times a day.

4. Redirect When Things Are Getting Off Track

If something isn't being done the way you want it to be— either small stuff or big stuff—do everyone a favor and redirect right away. Don't let things fester. And remember that your employee can't read your mind.

5. Focus on Solutions, Not Problems

When communicating to your employees about what isn't working for you, be sure to offer solutions and not just complaints. If you are consistently negative, people will eventually stop listening to you.

6. Communicate Expectations

At home, just as with your team at work, someone has to set the bar. At home, that's your job, so pay attention to every new issue (and there will be many with long-term employees) and establish how you want each one handled. Eventually, your employees will know what you expect from them.

7. Give Them Everything They Need to Do Their Jobs Well

This could be everything from petty cash to buying the right paint. The important thing is to arm your employees with all of the tools and supplies they need to do their jobs. We once had a dedicated cell phone for our babysitters. She would take it with her when she brought the kids outside so we knew they were reachable.

8. Don't Micromanage

Everyone thrives when they can get things done in their own way. Let them—at least with the smaller stuff.

9. Check In with Your Employee

Take time each week or sometimes each day to check in with your employee on how things are going. We have many friends who spend ten minutes each morning with their babysitter or day care center, reviewing the schedule and to-do list, but this can apply to everyone who works for you. If the person who mows your lawn shows up, spend a minute or two with him in order to find out how he is doing.

10. Set Goals and Objectives

We all thrive when we are working toward goals. Without them, many of us become unmotivated. No matter what the scope of the task or responsibility might be, work with your employees to set goals.

Hourly Employees
Who Make a Difference

It doesn't have to cost a fortune to free up a little time. Take a look at this list of inexpensive resources.

- *Babysitter*: Maybe you just need someone for a Saturday afternoon so you can work on your

planning, or a few hours after work so you have
the free time to swing by the bookstore or meet a
friend for coffee.

- *Lawn mower*: Depending on the size of your lawn,
mowing can take *hours*. Get that time back. It
doesn't cost much to hire someone to cut it,
maybe just twice a month.

- *House cleaner*: If you are overwhelmed by
the thought of changing sheets, cleaning out the
fridge, vacuuming the drapes, and polishing the
furniture, it might be time to hire a house cleaner.
Even having someone come in once a month to
vacuum and mop makes a big difference.

- *Accountant*: Even if you were a whiz with your
single tax return, things are a bit more
complicated now, aren't they? It is best to bring
in a professional. It might save you days of work,
not to mention money in the long run. And
if you have kept everything organized, then
you will save money on the hourly rate.

- *Bookkeeper*: Organizing your finances can be a
complicated, time-sucking endeavor. To get you
on the right track, enlist the help of a bookkeeper
to set up QuickBooks or a similar program. You
might even consider hiring her to come in
monthly to go over the books and clean up any
mistakes you may have made.

- *Dog walker*: If you don't have a backyard to let
  your dog run around in, then you are most likely
  going home midday to let your pet out. Or worse,
  you are making your dog wait eight or nine
  hours until your workday ends. We suggest
  hiring a dog walker for half an hour each workday
  to free up time and relieve guilt.

- *Teenagers*: Local teens twelve to fifteen years old
  are too young for most salaried jobs but might be
  ideal candidates to help you clean out the garage,
  run a tag sale, or gather bags of clothing for
  Goodwill.

- *Painters*: Because housepainters do most of their
  work in the summer, many of them need
  employment in the winter months. If you have
  been meaning to paint your kitchen or bedroom
  but don't have the time or expertise, contact a
  housepainter in his off-season.

- *Your kids! (if they're old enough)*: If your kids are old
  enough to follow instructions, then they might
  be old enough to "hire." Contribute to their
  allowance by assigning them jobs like raking
  leaves, shoveling snow, planting bulbs, or dusting
  the house. It's our opinion that kids should "earn"
  their allowance. There's a life lesson here: We
  adults all work for the money we need, so why
  not have your kids work the same way. It teaches

them to respect the money they earn and to feel good about the chores they do. They will see the direct correlation between doing something and getting paid for it.

True Story: Mom Plus Nanny Making It All Work

Katie is a single working mom of eight-year-old twins. Although she puts in long hours at her job as a director of a nonprofit foundation, she does have some flexibility during the week, including working from home on Fridays. But what makes her life doable (and manageable) is the full-time help of Jenna, the babysitter/house cleaner/pinch hitter who has worked for Katie since the kids were two years old. We spoke to Katie about how she works with Jenna in terms of setting schedules, dealing with conflicts and redirection, and the good and not-so-good parts of having a full-time employee in the home.

Managing at Home

One of the things that helps make things run smoothly between them is that Katie brings many of her professional management skills home. In her experience, the most important thing is to be "clear about roles and expectations." She agrees with us that many times we are too casual and informal with the people working in our household, because we leave those boundaries at work, but "this makes it confusing and frustrating for everyone." Being clear about the tasks—how you want them done and when you want them accomplished—is "crucial because it is a job that you are paying to have done." This is really no different from someone you manage at work. One action Katie takes to convey her expectations is giving Jenna a written document at the beginning of every school year. Katie "gives the hours, after-school programs, broad responsibilities, vacation time, and rate." Of course there is an understanding that there will be sick days, and Katie often lets Jenna go home early, but having this document "really helps us both understand what we are committing to and what the expectations are."

Being clear about the job and your expectations should start at the interview itself. Spending time outlining the specific tasks and details of the job will help both the employee and the employer have a positive working relationship.

Being a Good Boss

Katie shares that "there is a lot of overlap in my management style, but I think I'm a pretty easy boss in both places." Although she has "high expectations," she works "collaboratively with employees, including Jenna, to meet those expectations." At the office this may come across as somewhat rigid or harsh, but "when employees are doing their jobs well, I try to give them breaks and other positive feedback and perks frequently." Katie does this at home with Jenna as well. "I often let her leave early or give her days off when I am around." Katie also pays Jenna extra and fairly when she asks her to do things that are outside of her job responsibilities (e.g., walking the dog). With both her work and home employees, Katie is flexible about when they take time off to tend to personal matters. "In both cases, I think about the goodwill an employee earns and keeps in the bank—goodwill is earned by doing your job well, being trustworthy, and doing what you say."

In our experience, banking goodwill goes both ways. As the employer you need to demonstrate trust, appreciation, and support, and the employee needs to be responsible, responsive, and trustworthy. Each time you deliver on these promises, you are strengthening your working relationships.

Tweaking the Job Description

At the office, when you have long-term employees, they most likely have been promoted several times and you have worked closely with them to change their responsibilities during each promotion. It is no different at home when your household's needs change. Katie experienced this when her boys started going to school full-time and she knew that Jenna's role would be less as a babysitter and more as a housekeeper. "The spring before they started, I could see she was nervous about my letting her go. We sat down and I had written out for her what I thought I would need moving forward. I explained that the job would be more housekeeper, running errands, etc., versus babysitter, and then asked her if she was comfortable doing that kind of work." Katie made sure that Jenna knew that whatever her answer, it was fine and that she was loved and cared about regardless of her interest in staying. The important thing is that Katie engaged Jenna in the process and asked her directly if she wanted a new job—because essentially it was. For Katie the important thing was "being clear about the expectations of this new job and being explicit."

Too often when the needs of your household change, you tend to tiptoe through the transition, being vague about the new job description and the expectations. Maybe it's guilt or fear of disappointing the employee, but if you are not clear, then both parties will end up resentful. The employer will feel like she isn't getting what she needs and the employee will feel used.

If you are new to hiring someone for your household, you need to know that your first employee might not work out and that's okay. Like many things in life, it's helpful to learn what you don't want, because that will help you define what you do want. In Katie's case, she added "cooking" to Jenna's list, having been frustrated with a nanny who refused to help her prepare meals for the boys. "Even though she was an excellent babysitter, I ended up spending every Sunday night making food for the week. This was really disappointing because food was really important to me, but I just didn't have time to run home and make dinner for all of us to enjoy. I knew when interviewing Jenna that I was looking for someone who wanted to be a part of the household, not just take care of the boys during the day."

This is an important lesson, because the person who fits into your household the best might not be the most obvious candidate on paper. When you are interviewing, make sure you share some of the values that are important to you. In Katie's case, she spoke to Jenna about how she looked forward to sitting down and eating with the boys as a family and how she would need Jenna's help to make that happen.

When You Can't Afford More Raises

Jenna has been with Katie so long that she is now at the top of the pay scale, and it just wouldn't make financial sense for Kate to pay her more money. To guarantee that this doesn't become a source of tension between them, Katie sat down with Jenna and explained the situation and assured her it was no reflection on her performance. In addition to "very large Christmas bonuses," Katie now rewards Jenna with extra days off.

Financial realities are what they are. If you can't responsibly give your employee another raise, then sit down and discuss it with him, offer to make up for it in other ways, and let it be known that you accept and respect his choice to stay or to go.

Strengthening your home team is just the beginning of shoring up things at home. In the following chapter we'll show you what else you can do to plan better and protect your family against any potential rough patches.

good days, bad days

PREPARING FOR, AVOIDING, AND CELEBRATING LIFE'S BUMPS

Companies with foresight have a document they hope never to open: a crisis manual that outlines what to do in all sorts of emergencies. For food companies, it details the steps required during a salmonella outbreak. For toy companies, it delineates the actions to take in case of a recall. For banks, it features a communications plan for getting the word out about a computer glitch. These manuals offer us an important lesson: No company, no matter how big or well organized, is totally immune from a crisis; it's how it *responds* to the crisis that matters most.

The same is true for a home. Even the most organized, tightly run household can be faced with an unexpected situation—a layoff, an illness, or even a death—big enough to rock your foundation, unless you're adequately prepared. In fact, unlike a company, which can theoretically go forever without a crisis, it's all but certain that a family will face at least a handful of both big and small challenges over its lifetime.

The section entitled "Your Support Team" will explain how having personal relationships with a lawyer, an accountant, a doctor, a bank officer, a responsible neighbor, and a veterinarian can help you be prepared to deal with adversity. With the help of a personal finance expert, we'll show you how to determine how much you should have in an emergency fund and things to consider when building one. You'll find a template for a household one-sheet that highlights key contact information and directions for how to handle an emergency, which anyone in your house might need to reference if you are not home or are not reachable in case of a medical emergency or accident. You'll also hear the true story of a family that learned to look on the bright side of a layoff. You will read a Q&A with an insurance broker who will help you determine if long-term disability is a good idea and how to identify a life insurance plan that will truly protect those you love. We believe that although this chapter addresses topics nobody wants to contemplate, the benefits of being prepared far outweigh the perils of ignoring the realities of life.

Something Happens to Everyone

There is nobody alive who hasn't encountered adversity during her lifetime. Some dramas are life-changing, some are just disruptive, and most are unavoidable. But while the situations may be unavoidable, you can have things in place to protect you and your family from additional harm and distress. In our case, we had a series of personal and professional setbacks in 2011 that left us gleefully turning the page at midnight on December 31. We'll spare you the details, but suffice it to say that the challenges we faced over the course of the year included illness, financial strain, and a family death. While we look back on those twelve months and accept that we couldn't do anything about the illness or the passing away of a loved one, we could have had a better handle on our finances than we did at the time. When a client stiffed Caitlin for almost $15,000 of back pay and pulled out of a yearlong agreement with zero notice, we were left scrambling to replace that income and had a full-on anxiety attack. It turned out it was a totally avoidable anxiety attack.

If we had only taken a few steps to protect ourselves with an emergency fund, we would have been able to buy time to figure out what to do next. Instead, we entered the summer—a time in our businesses when it's almost impossible to line up work—in a bad way. Now, it all ended up fine, we sold a few projects, Caitlin was hired for a consulting gig, and our debts were paid off. But it was a hard five months where we spent more time juggling accounts and stressing out than enjoying what turned out to be an unexpected summer off with the kids. When things were back to normal and we had healthy bank accounts again, we went back to the basics, looking at everything we could do now to protect ourselves from something surprising us again. We hope that when you read through this chapter, you will take some of our advice and protect yourselves too.

True Story: Changing Roles Can Be Great for the Family

We heard through the grapevine that Stephen, a friend of ours, had lost his job during a massive layoff at a fairly large financial company. We reached out to take him to lunch, and at that time he was anxious and frustrated about his situation. He told us that his family hadn't prepared for something like this happening, since he always made a lot of money. Losing his job had forced them to start considering major life changes, including pulling his kids out of private school and selling the weekend home that they loved. We know that these aren't the issues that most of us face and that our friend was really pretty lucky to have these kinds of problems, but still, losing your income is scary for anybody. That isn't why we included him in the book, however. About a month after our lunch, we called to check in with Stephen and he seemed pretty happy. No, he hadn't found a job, but his wife had gotten a great consulting job that resulted in their roles changing significantly. And he kind of liked it. So we spoke to Stephen about how a crisis had given him a new perspective on his family and household.

Preparing

Unlike most of the other couples we interviewed, who were financially prepared to lose their jobs, Stephen's family was not. They had very high expenses, including covering the costs of two homes and three private-school tuitions. Luckily for them, they were emotionally prepared for the layoff, since Stephen's industry had been changing so radically. He also noted that as a family, they "have become much more cautious and much more frugal but remain optimistic and stay away from doomsday scenarios."

We strongly encourage you to be both financially and emotionally prepared for change. Even if you are never laid off, it's better for about a million reasons to have an emergency fund available should some unexpected crisis come up. Healthy companies always plan for change and challenges. Chief financial officers often look ahead one to five years to protect the company with smart investments and healthy bank accounts.

Shifting Responsibilities

Stephen used to work seriously long hours, travel for business, and attend late-night work events—in short, he wasn't really around. These days his role at home has changed enormously. Stephen told us, "I have become an active participant in every aspect of our family life as opposed to a spectator who hears about it all on the phone, in an e-mail, or gets caught up on the weekends." He now "takes the kids to school, picks them up, helps arrange and coordinate playdates, liaises with the teachers, goes on class trips, attends sporting events, helps with homework and long-term projects, does the grocery shopping, and makes dinner."

But does he like the shift in responsibilities? "I love having the opportunity to play an active role in my kids' lives and get firsthand experience and knowledge of who they really are and who they are becoming."

Enjoy the unexpected gifts that come along with life changes. Stephen has been given a special opportunity to reconnect with his family and luckily he knows that and is appreciating it.

Using Work Skills at Home

Since Stephen has a very impressive résumé and has held executive positions, we asked him what work skills were cropping up in his new role at home. He started with delegation: "It is essential when it comes to table setting and table clearing." He also sets "specific goals for what time playdates begin and end, with insistence on clear and solid communication before, during, and after." He sets up goals up front with "rewards [for meeting the goals] or consequences for missing the set goals." Stephen has also "reorganized most of the closets in the kitchen and general living spaces, moving on to each kid's room next." But he isn't always the best manager. "I will say that I never raised my voice or lost control with a colleague at work—not so easy at home. My home colleagues are much better at pushing buttons and disobeying directives."

We love that Stephen hasn't left his workplace skills behind him—not only because we consider work skills to be life skills, but also because it will make Stephen's transition back to the workplace easier if he keeps up his management and organizational mojo.

Good and Bad

We spoke to Stephen about the upside of the changing roles, and he told us that what he loves the most is how it benefits the family. "I love helping my wife and freeing her up mentally and physically to do her job and of course spending time with my kids." He also likes that he has been able to put in extra time and energy with his favorite charity. As far as the downside, he could do without the guilt. "I have a lot of trouble handling the guilt I feel for not producing revenue, not being an active member of the workforce, of not being creative in a business environment, of not moving my career forward." Stephen also feels guilty about the downtime and has trouble balancing constant job-related research with interviews and kid-related activities.

Stephen does "enjoy the rewards of self-accomplishment regarding the kids and the home" but misses the collaborative nature of the workplace. "I have an optimist's crazy feeling that the next gig is around the corner."

Our advice to Stephen and to everyone out there who is letting guilt get the best of them: Don't! You can only control so much, and if you are doing your best to get life back on track, then at least enjoy yourself in the process.

Shoring Up Starts with the Basics

When protecting yourself from last-minute dramas, you want to start by assessing the state of your small stuff. We're going to get into the wills and retirement planning later, but for now let's act as your company's head of operations and look at the systems, equipment, and building that keep things running. We want to look under the hood of your car and on top of the roof of your house, because small fixes and extended warranties will save you major financial headaches later on.

Equipment/Appliances

We read once that you should have a one-sheet that lists all of your major appliances, including their model numbers, serial numbers, a note about the expiration date of the warranty, the manufacturer's phone number, and a local repair service. It may be a little extreme to take the time to do this, but at the end of this exercise you will have a better idea of any potential issues that may crop up in the near future. If your washing machine is ten years old and no longer under warranty, then you may be looking at needing a replacement soon. Make sure to service things like your lawn mower and computers—it will be less expensive than replacing them.

Automobile

What shape is it in? Does it need a tune-up? Oil change? Should you rustproof the undercarriage? Is there anything you can do now to extend the life of the car? For instance, if you have a windshield chip, get it fixed ASAP because it can lead to a full crack, which will cost around $1,000 to repair. Does the car still meet your needs, or is it time to trade it in for a larger (or smaller) model?

House: Interior

Walk through the house and take notes of what needs fixing. Cracked windows that need replacing? Raised floorboards that need to be reset? Closet doors that need readjusting? Is the plumbing system working properly? Is the heating system doing its job? What about the security system? Are there dings in the wall that need to be patched or missing grout in the bathtub?

House: Exterior

Does your house need repainting or do you have a few years? How is the roof? The gutters? Again, is there anything that you should be doing now to avoid a major expense down the road? If you are unsure what you are looking for, you might consider hiring an inspector to walk through the house with you and give you a better idea of its state.

Looking at the condition of your house and your things doesn't take a lot of time, but it does take focus. Ultimately, having things updated and serviced will save you time and money down the road.

Your Professional Health

There are a billion career books on the market (Caitlin has written several of them!), so we aren't going to go into what you can do at work to protect your job. Rather we are going to focus on protecting yourself should you lose your job. Even if you are excelling at work and love what you do, it is always smart to keep an updated résumé on hand because you *never* know what is around the corner. You could meet someone at a party who mentions a job that you have always wanted to have, you could be laid off because your company has changed direction, or you could suddenly find yourself with a new boss you can't stand. Even if nothing happens and no new opportunities worth pursuing present themselves, it is better to be prepared for change.

In addition to having an up-to-date résumé, make sure

that you maintain and develop your network. Caitlin has a friend who has worked at the same company for twenty-five years. He has held a variety of positions within the organization and at this point is the number two. But he only knows the people at the company, having spent zero time cultivating his network. This is a really big mistake and a missed opportunity because he has the clout in his current position to meet new, influential people. New people come with new ideas and new opportunities. So not only is he not growing as a professional but, should he be laid off, he will have no one to turn to for advice or potential jobs. He will have to rely on a headhunter, which, as we know, is often not how you land the perfect job. So don't be like Caitlin's friend. Protect your future by growing your safety net of contacts. Take people out to lunch, check in around the holidays, invite people out for an after-work drink, and go to professional conferences and other gatherings. Offer to give people advice, pass along job leads, and in every way possible become an active and engaged member in your professional community.

Your Financial Health

By now you have a good idea of how much you have in your checking, savings, and retirement accounts, but do you have enough of a buffer to protect yourself against a major or even minor financial setback? We have two friends who both went through layoffs within a week of each other. They were both the major breadwinners for their families, which increased the seriousness of their situations. Cheri was laid off with only a month's savings in the bank. She also hadn't done the preparation work we talked about in the previous section regarding her résumé and network, so she was already behind when it came to looking for another job. Six weeks of white-knuckle stress forced her to accept a position that was below her experience and pay grade. David, on the other hand, had worked hard with his wife, Jen, to have six months' worth of savings in the bank. He also had a résumé ready to go out and a robust network of people willing to meet with him. When we asked him why he had so much savings, he said he knew that the possibility of a layoff was significant and that as a senior-level person, it would take longer to get a job. So his four months of looking, while stressful, was something they could live with, and it gave him the time to find the right job, which turned out to be . . . working for himself.

So let's talk about an emergency savings account. Having money set aside in a "just in case" fund is a hard thing to commit to when dollars are already stretched. But, even when the job market is healthy, it's always better to have a cushion for yourself, your family, and any loved ones who may need your help one day. An emergency fund isn't just there in case of a lost income—it can also help cover expenses that crop up if someone gets seriously ill or some other crisis ensues.

How Much Should You Have in an Emergency Account?

The rule of thumb used to be to have an emergency savings fund that would cover at least three months' worth of expenses. But since the crash of 2008, experts advise that having six months' worth of expenses should be the minimum. This isn't just because it's harder to find a new job in a tough economy; it's also because credit companies are putting restrictions on their loaning policies and falling housing prices have decreased how much you can borrow against your property. There is just less credit available out there, even if you have an excellent credit score. The only thing you can rely on absolutely being there when you need it is cash. So start saving it.

Savings Basics

Pull out your budget and start calculating how much you need to live on for six months. If there are big annual payments like the renewal on your life insurance policy or your property tax, then fold it into this number. Better to work toward saving more than you need than being caught short. Don't pass out when you see how big that nut looks. It's going to be a lot of money, but remember that any money in the bank is better than none. The important thing is to be committed and to get started saving today.

First things first: gather the low-hanging fruit. In other words, there are places you can painlessly save. To find them, spend one week tracking every single penny you spend. Buy a notebook or use the note function on your smartphone and record that $1.50 you spent on a pack of gum, the 50 cents you put into the meter, and the $3.75 you spent on the decaf latte. At the end of the week you will see many, many places to save. Bring lunch a few times a week and put that $20 into your account, drink the coffee they have in the office instead of running out to Starbucks and that's another $10 into your savings.

Then there are the places to save that may require a few phone calls or a little time. We switched our car insurance and saved hundreds of dollars a year. Consider a family plan for cell phones, find a lower-interest-rate credit card, or join a membership wholesale club, such as Costco or BJ's.

You get the point.

Ten More Places to Save

1. If your prescriptions are costing you a fortune, see if you can use your insurance to order them online through a company like Medco. For those of you who regularly take medication, you can save a lot since you can buy them in bulk.

2. Use those credit card rewards points to get gift cards at retailers you frequent. Use the gift cards to buy things you need, or keep them for holiday gifts.

3. Oil is a fortune these days. It costs almost twice what it did five years ago to heat your home. Since you most likely aren't in a position to put up the solar panels right now, take a few hours one fall weekend and winterize your home. Putting plastic on drafty windows, sealing up unused doors, and caulking those drafty holes will keep your house warmer while bringing your heating costs down. You can always wear warm sweaters rather than turning up the heat.

4. If you need to replace a computer, you might want to look into a refurbished machine rather than shell out the money for a new one.

5. Stock up when things go out of season. This holds true for clothing, gardening supplies, and of course decorations (think of all those Christmas sales).

6. Buy gifts all year long. We all come across great sales throughout the year. So next time you see the perfect gift for your aunt Liz in July, buy it and you'll save time and money during the hectic holiday season.

7. When it comes to grocery shopping, there are tons of ways to save money. Buy in season for starters. Buy things like potatoes and onions in bags; they are significantly less expensive than buying them a few at a time. Buy the things you use a lot (toilet paper, paper towels, shampoo, bath soap, laundry detergent, ground meats, juice boxes) in bulk. Don't be a frozen food snob; most of it was frozen at the peak of freshness and items like seafood are less expensive this way. Consider joining a food co-op: You will most likely need to commit a little time to helping it run, but the quality of the food will be better and cheaper.

8. Your car needs a repair. Don't go with the first mechanic you speak to. Just like you would with any major purchase, get a few estimates before hiring someone. We were just told that our car needed a repair to the catalytic converter that would cost us about $600. We spoke to another mechanic, slightly out of the way, who said he would charge us $300 less. Was it worth the hour drive? Yes.

9. Rather than hiring a babysitter for a Saturday night, consider setting up an arrangement with friends whereby you trade off watching the kids for date nights. Chances are the kids will have more fun, too.

10. Instead of driving everywhere (gas is a fortune), revisit public transportation. In many cities and even large towns, public transportation is a viable and even convenient option.

About Your Debt

Protecting yourself from financial trouble includes reducing the amount of personal debt you carry. Take a look at what you owe and add a line item into your budget to pay it down. We are focusing on the bad debt right now, not the student loans or mortgage payments that are part of the cost of living (in our opinion). So look at your credit card statement and you might see a chart that will tell you how much you need to pay monthly to get the balance paid off in five, ten, fifteen, or twenty years. Commit to a time to pay it off and make sure you pay that new minimum payment, not the one listed on your bill. We have gone through periods where we owed no money on credit cards and times where we owed too much. It can be disheartening to pay significant amounts of money, but you will feel better once you take control of it and start chipping away at the debt. Please, don't stop contributing to your savings account while paying off your debt. You can do both, but it might take a little longer.

Debt Reduction in Four Steps

- Step One: Cut up the cards and do not sign up
  for more.

- Step Two: Figure out how much you owe and to whom you owe it.
- Step Three: Make a chart that looks something like this . . .

Lender	Amount Owed	Interest Rate	Yearly Interest Payment

This will show you how much you pay on just the interest alone.

- Step Four: There are two different schools of thought on which credit card to pay off first, so here they both are. The first school believes that you should pick your biggest debt (credit card or car loan) to pay off. While you are paying the minimum payment on the other cards, send extra payments to this one. The thinking is that your biggest debt costs you more each month on the interest payments, so you want it gone. The second option is to pay off the smallest debt first because there are some lenders who will look at not just how much you owe but how many cards you have.

Your Retirement Health

No, we aren't talking about your cholesterol level, we are talking about your savings plan for retirement. Way back in the day, you used to be able to count on Social Security payments to cover your expenses and Medicare to take care of your health needs. No longer. Now it's on individuals to control the financial planning for their retirement. And we are living longer, on average until eighty-four years old. This means that if you are planning on retiring at sixty-five, you will need to save a significant amount of money. In addition, there have been several articles in places including *The Wall Street Journal* that look at how living longer is going to affect our health care needs. According to the experts interviewed, those extra years mean that we are going to be dealing with chronic illnesses like diabetes that call for costly medications. Since insurance companies are busy cutting back on how much and what they cover, this means that retirees will have to go out of pocket to pay for many of these medications. What can you do? Since we don't have a crystal ball and can't know for certain what the future role of the federal government or state government is going to be in our health care, we can only prepare for the worst and set aside additional money in our retirement accounts to cover prescriptions. Experts suggest saving in the neighborhood of $6,000 a year just to cover those out-of-pocket expenses that aren't covered by insurance. The good news is that the sooner you start setting aside money for retirement, the more your interest will accumulate, and the more you will have.

A Few Basic Tips for Retirement Planning

1. Figure Out How Much You Need

   The quickest way to figure out this number is by taking your existing monthly expenses and then hopping online to find a retirement calculator (cnn.com, Bloomberg.com, aarp.org) to plug them into. Think through each line item before adding them to the retirement calculator, because not all of them will apply. You most likely won't have to pay for child care when you are retired, so you can cut that. You can bring down the amount you spend on clothing and groceries, because your household will be smaller. You may want to bring up the numbers you have on there for travel, medical expenses, recreation, and entertainment. Experts say you will need 60 to 85 percent of today's annual income to live on when you retire.

2. Start Saving, Keep Saving,
   and Leave the Money Alone

All of the experts we spoke to said the key to painless retirement planning is starting early. If you
haven't, start today! Once you have the accounts
set up, leave them alone and let the money grow.
If you start borrowing the money, then you may
have tax liability issues to deal with.

3. Enroll in Your Company's Retirement Plan

The easiest first step is to sign up for your
company's 401(k) plan, because most likely they
match your contributions and that's free money.
Caitlin was recently eligible to enroll in her company's 401(k) and couldn't believe how quickly her
account built up thanks to the matching contribution. Promise yourself that if you haven't done
this yet, reach out to your HR contact tomorrow.
It's found money.

4. Get Help

Next up, find a reputable financial planner to help
you outline an action plan for retirement savings.
They will look at your financial big picture—what

you owe, what your goals are, your age, the ages of your children—and determine how much you should be setting aside each month. As for where to find a good one, ask your accountant first and make sure you check their references before hiring them.

5. Sign Up for an IRA

In addition to your company 401(k), we want to encourage you to open an Individual Retirement Account (IRA). There are tax advantages and you can contribute up to $5,000 a year into these accounts, or more if you are older than fifty.

6. Find Out About Your Company's Pension Funds

Ask your employer if you are eligible for a pension. If you are, then find out the details.

7. Figure Out Your Social Security Benefits

Find out what your Social Security benefits will be and factor that in your planning. Try to start taking the money as late as you can. Waiting until you are seventy-two to tap into this benefit could mean you will have thousands of dollars more to draw from.

8. Save More Money Than You Think You Will Need

Remember to factor inflation into your number and set a goal to save more than you need, because we just don't know what things are going to cost when we retire. We also don't know how long we'll live.

9. Stay on Top of Your Investments

Diversify your accounts, don't be too conservative with your investments too early, and get professional guidance to make sure that your money is growing safely.

10. Keep an Eye Out for "Passive" Savings

By "passive" savings, we mean little bits of stock or forgotten IRAs that are just sitting there not earning anything. It's usually better to combine these types of accounts. We have a friend who just found an old 401(k) statement from a former job and realized she had $1,500 just sitting there.

Your Support Team

In this world of HMOs, e-mails, and automated phone systems, where it's next to impossible to speak to someone directly for a quick answer or advice, we strongly recommend pulling together a handful of professionals with whom you have a personal relationship: results-oriented experts with whom you can make an appointment or, at the very least, get on the phone to help you resolve a crisis. Just to be clear, we're not suggesting anything as drastic as having, say, an attorney on retainer. But establishing a relationship with the following experts— even if it means just introducing yourself by phone or e-mail, and paving the way for contact should the need arise—can be invaluable. All of the members of your support team should be chosen for their *ability*, *accessibility*, and *affordability*.

Your support team should include:

Attorney: Waiting until a messy legal situation crops up is *not* the time to begin the search for a lawyer. Hopefully, you'll never need to call on the advice of counsel, but easy access to one is essential in these litigious times. (While we're on the subject, if you haven't already prepared one, you both really should have a will, though you will want to enlist an attorney who specializes in estate planning for this unpleasant but essential document.)

Accountant: An audit, the IRS disputing your
refund, the need to file an extension—all good
reasons to have an accountant. You also might
think about turning the preparation of your tax
return over to a CPA, because often she can
find so many deductions that might elude you
that they pay for themselves and still save you
money.

Bank Officer: Should you need a line of credit, or
encounter an error on your statement, having the
card of a helpful bank officer is a godsend.

General Practitioner: Do you really want to trust
the advice of an ER intern if a medical emergency
occurs? Have a general practitioner who is willing
to give you his cell phone number or be paged by
his service in case of a crisis. And go in once a year
for an annual physical—the best way to avoid a
health-related emergency.

Financial Adviser: If you have been laid off, or for
some reason need to liquidate your IRA, then an
accessible and responsible financial adviser will
come in handy. (For example, she might point out
that you can *borrow* against your IRA for sixty

days with no tax liability or penalty, something you might not have realized on your own.)

Neighbor: Over the course of the three years that we have lived in our neighborhood, we have come close to depending on our neighbor Joe. He helped move our car when we were out of town, watched our daughter when she was sick and we couldn't get home fast enough to pick her up from school—even came over to help Caitlin when she found a dying mouse in our pantry. And yes, we help him out when he needs it. The point is that a reliable, trustworthy, responsible neighbor that you can give a set of your house keys to is a gift.

From the Desk of . . .

Tara Benstead has been a financial adviser for almost a decade and has worked with individuals and small business owners. She is currently focusing on individuals in education, local government, and county government and their families. She stresses the importance of retirement planning and saving for retirement to her clients, but she also offers insurance and investment products to fit financial goals in the short and intermediate term. She tells us that she wants to get people thinking about retirement no matter what age they are. For obvious reasons, we thought she would be the perfect person to speak to about retirement planning. We thought it most helpful for you if we quoted our interview from Tara in its entirety. We found her advice incredibly useful and hope that you do, too.

Retirement planning is something we all hear about but are often unsure where to begin. What are the first steps people should take to start laying the groundwork for a healthy retirement savings?

Retirement planning is becoming increasingly important as both men and women are living longer and spending more years in retirement. The first and most important step is to get started. It is never too late, and as an adviser, I say that a lot.

The second step is finding an adviser to work with. In retirement planning, it is crucial to find an adviser that you are comfortable working with. Too often people think they can do it themselves. When I have a plumbing issue in my home, I call a plumber.

When I am sick, I go to the doctor. With your finances, you should always have a trusted adviser (or two, or three) whom you work with. You will not always "get it right" the first time, and do not let this discourage you. Many times, family and friends or even coworkers can refer you to someone they trust. Ask around. You do not have to discuss your finances or let your friends know what you are looking to do with an adviser; just ask if they have a financial adviser that they trust.

The third step is to set your goals. This process may require that you do a little homework, and most of the time this will be with the help of an adviser. When I initially meet with someone, I ask a lot of questions, questions that you may have never considered. If you could stop working and be financially independent, at what age would you do so? Will you continue to work in some capacity, even if it is just to keep busy, or will you be golfing every day, vacationing, traveling the world? I want to know where you are today and where you want to be. The most important part here is to be open. Everyone is different and has different goals. You are unique and your financial and retirement planning should reflect this. There is no single answer for everyone. There are plenty of tools and calculators available online, and some are better than others, but the best tool you can have is an adviser that works with you.

Take a look at your current budget and spending. Be honest with yourself. Write it all down. You can do a Google search for budget worksheets if you need help brainstorming for things you normally don't consider, and a good adviser will help you create and work out a budget that fits your needs. Then think about how things will change, or how you want them to change, in retirement. Will your mortgage be paid off? Will you travel more? Will you move out of state, downsize, or live at the beach? And then do another budget (or make a second column in your budget) for retirement. You are working with today's dollars, but an adviser will be able to help you factor inflation into your plan to show you what it will cost to maintain your lifestyle any number of years down the road.

Next, you want to take an inventory of your progress toward your retirement goals. Have you saved anything for retirement yet? Do you have a 401(k) or other employer-sponsored retirement plan at work or from a previous job? Will you be eligible for a pension? Social Security? Do you have faith that it will be there for you? This is a factor I typically let my clients decide. Whether I believe that it will be there for them or not is not important. If they are counting on it being available, we plug it into the equation; if not, we leave it out.

Now that you have made the important decision to get started, you have found an adviser to work with, you have taken a hard look at your current budget and expenses and given some thought to how this is going to change for you in retirement, you will have a better idea of how much you need to save in order to reach those goals. The farther away you are from retirement, generally speaking, the smaller the amount you will need to put away each month/week/year to reach your goals. The closer you are to that date, the more you will need to save. Risk is also going to play a part in how much you need to save. The more risk you are willing to take, the more potential you have for higher returns over time. This doesn't mean that you must take risk to save for retirement. The important thing is saving. An adviser will work with you to determine your risk tolerance and educate you on the risks in the market and the risks in retirement. He will determine what types of investments will best suit your needs and goals.

The next step would be to determine what vehicle to use for your savings. There are IRAs, Roth IRAs, employer sponsored plans, mutual funds, annuities, stocks—the possibilities are endless, and each has its own unique advantages. The best way to determine which is best for you is to work with your adviser.

Once you have started saving in one of these vehicles, you want to continue to add to them on a regular basis, and review the investment allocation and how the savings are doing relative to your goals on a regular basis, at least annually, with your adviser.

What if people are behind or lost most of what they had invested in 2008?

The market can be intimidating and scary, but do not let this discourage you from planning and saving. The most common mistake that I see my clients make is stopping their investments when the market goes down, as it did in 2008–2009. As backward as it sounds, when the market is down, it is really an opportunity to buy the same investments you have been purchasing at a lower price. Our emotions sometimes cloud our investment decisions and cause us to react quickly without taking a step back to think about what we should do. This is another reason why having an adviser is so important. I always tell my clients to call me if they ever feel uncomfortable, have a question or concern, or are questioning our strategy.

For those who are behind or lost a lot in 2008, if you stayed invested in the market, the news is good because you have probably recovered a lot of your losses. For those who sold out of the market into fixed or lower-risk investments, it may take a while to recover what you lost. The important thing in both scenarios is to take this time to reevaluate your personal plan. There is no right or wrong answer, so no matter which move you did or did not make, you can still plan for the future. The year 2008 was a good test of risk tolerance. Some people who thought they were comfortable with more aggressive portfolios had a reality check, and this can be used going forward with your investments.

What would you tell people who haven't started their retirement savings and are now in their thirties, forties, or fifties?

Whether you are in your forties or you lost the bulk of your savings in 2008, you can still work toward your goals in retirement. Think about the things that are in your control and that you are willing to change and what things you are not. You can control how much you save and, barring an unforeseen accident or health issue, how long you are willing to work. How much do you spend leading up to and in retirement? You cannot control the market, you cannot control tax rates, and you cannot control how long you live. So ask yourself: "Am I willing to work a few more years in order to reach my goals? Am I willing to save another one hundred to two hundred dollars a month now if it means I can retire at the age I want? Am I willing to go out to eat one time less per month and put that money toward my retirement savings?"

Worst-Case Scenarios

Wills and Living Wills

We don't want to come off as all doom and gloom in this chapter, we really don't. We just want you to think about the "what-ifs" so you aren't caught unprepared and unprotected. In the event that something dire happens to you or your partner, you absolutely must have a will. A will is more than just a document outlining where you want your things to go. It can provide instructions for how and where you want to be buried and your preferences for who you want to raise your children and how you want them raised. It can answer the tough, complicated questions for your partner. A living will is a document that gives your instructions should an event make you unable to make decisions on your own behalf. Both of these documents are gifts to the ones you have left behind—essential paperwork that will give you peace of mind as you live your life. As for who can write one up for you, it is best to go with a lawyer.

Life Insurance

Another absolute must. If you have children, you owe it to them to have a life insurance policy that will ensure that they will continue living the quality of life that you have established for them as a living parent. We both have life insurance policies that will cover the care of our children, their housing, and their college. Of course, we don't expect to have to use them, but we need them.

Godparents

You will most likely be asked this question by the professional preparing your will, but please spend a lot of time thinking about who in your life will be able to love, guide, and parent your children in the manner that you would. We had a very hard time with this decision because it's heartbreaking to think about, but once we identified the couple and spoke to them about the role we wanted them to take, we felt a thousand times better.

Insurance

Some of us are insurance-crazy these days, but seriously, how can you not be? Things happen and it's better to be covered than caught off guard. There are some insurance policies that are required by law (automobile insurance) and some that should be (home owner's insurance/rental insurance). There are supplemental health insurance plans, insurance for your boats, jewelry, and, in the case of certain celebrities, legs. You can insure almost anything. Determining what to insure and for how much is both a practical and a personal decision. We want to encourage you to meet with a broker like Eric Robinson (interviewed next), a straight shooter who will help you identify what you should, need, and want to have coverage for.

From the Desk of . . .

Eric Robinson is the president of PSC Insurance in New York City. He specializes in helping families and small businesses protect their health, wealth, and assets in the most tax-efficient and cost-effective manner possible. When Caitlin co-owned the public relations company, Eric helped her set up a health insurance policy to cover the handful of employees who worked there, and then when she went out on her own she used Eric to set up a new health insurance policy for her family. Now she uses Eric to help with rental insurance. He has helped us in many stages of our lives, and his advice has always proven to be sound.

The Most Important Insurance to Have

With absolute certainty, Eric tells us that "health insurance is the most important insurance to have," but you need to protect yourself by asking a lot of questions. "You need to ask a health care provider if they take your insurance, how much the co-pay is, how much a test or procedure is going to cost. Then you have to call your insurance company and confirm everything." It's true that people are afraid of asking about networks and coverage, but you have to ask because the direction that health care companies are going in means that they are looking to cover in-network-only doctors and hospitals. Eric says, "We've been conditioned to think that everything is covered by your insurance company and all we have to do is hand over our card, but that isn't true anymore." He encourages us to be "smarter consumers" by doing research and asking questions with confidence. You have the right to know how much something is going to cost you before moving forward.

"I have an example for you," Eric said. "Because the world is moving to in-network providers only, we assume we are covered everywhere and we're not. With the world of HMOs and regional networks, it's very possible while you are vacationing in Massachusetts, the only place you may have health care coverage is if you went to an emergency room. You have emergency room coverage everywhere. But it could be the in-network deductible plus the co-pay." Better to know what you have, how and where it works than to get stuck with a bunch of unexpected bills.

Home Owner's Insurance Is Essential

Eric believes that everyone should have some type of home owner's insurance and it doesn't matter if you own or rent. "The primary reason you want that coverage is not to satisfy the bank or landlord but to protect you against liability issues." The good news is that rental insurance is very, very inexpensive, Eric said, in the $200-to-$500 range. "Home insurance does a few things for you. First and foremost, it protects your stuff. But it also protects you against liability." Let's face it—we live in a litigious society, and if your umbrella pulls out of your hands and hits someone and knocks their teeth out, then you could get sued for negligence. Of course that scenario is ridiculous, but Eric assured us that "your little policy will follow you around so that person will be fighting your insurance company, not you." It's essential and it's cheap enough that everyone should have it.

Disability Insurance Explained

Disability insurance basically protects your ability to make a living. If you can't work, the insurance company will pay you. If you have a good policy and you become disabled either permanently or temporarily, insurance will give you monthly income tax-free. Eric explains that "there is group disability, which you get through your job, and it's generally taxable because the company is providing it as a benefit." You can also buy it individually, which generally isn't taxable, but you'll have to pay for it. Why is it important to have disability? Eric reminds us that disability "protects your most important asset—not your house, not your *car, not your 401(k), but your ability to get up and go to work."*

A Few Thoughts on Life Insurance

Eric reminds us, "Life insurance basically allows your spouse to continue in the lifestyle that the two of you enjoyed without the other person. It's bad enough to lose a spouse, and it's worse if everything else goes down the tubes as well." Your life can become difficult really quickly without life insurance. When loved ones pass away, everyone wants their money and they don't care about your loss. The money helps you cope with the situation.

In-Home Accidents

We asked Eric to talk to us about what protects a family if the nanny slips and falls. "If a contractor is in your house and hurts himself, your home owner's insurance would protect you." But he does recommend asking everyone who works in or on your home (plumbers, contractors, roofers, painters) to provide proof of their insurance. "If anyone is doing major work—like a renovation—you want to be named as an additional insured. They can write to their insurance company and ask them to send a copy of liability coverage. So if they are working on a wall and it ruins your neighbor's wall, you are covered."

As for a nanny who has slipped, "Technically, in most states by law you are required to provide worker's compensation and statutory disability insurance. It is no different from having an employee. Nannies not on the books are a liability." One of the easiest ways to address this is to use a payroll service. They charge you a monthly fee but will file all of this paperwork for you. You can then have access to workers' comp and disability insurance.

We hope that you see the value in planning ahead and you don't wrap up this chapter thinking we are two people who expect the worst. Rather, we are two people who have been through some difficult times without a safety net. Some of the life changes we suggest you make are hard ones, and yes, there will be some conflict. To help guide you through these periods of tension, we have included advice in the following chapter on conflict resolution.

we need to talk

CONFLICT RESOLUTION

Let's be honest: No matter how much advice they're given, couples will still have disagreements. But even when it comes to confrontations, the ways of the office offer solutions for the home. It's been our experience that approaching conflicts—especially those induced by stress—in a more businesslike manner helps reduce the tension in any discussion, and reducing the anger, fury, and frustration inherent in any argument is the first step toward finding a resolution that works for everybody.

Many offices have very strict codes of behavior when it comes to conflict; for example, if you are having problems with a coworker, there is usually a manager or human resources representative to talk to about it. It's only the occasional unhinged or irate boss who gets to scream. Since at home there isn't a professional trained in conflict resolution sitting in your living room, you need to take on this role yourselves. The advice throughout this chapter will help you identify issues before they blow up, and it will demonstrate how to resolve a disagreement as quickly and as painlessly as possible.

Throughout the pages of this chapter, you will find tips for understanding your partner's point of view without giving up your own, ways to let your partner know that you "hear" the other side of the issue, and how to state needs without losing your temper. An interview with Dr. Gary Schuman, a corporate leadership consultant, will offer practical advice for having a productive resolution meeting at home. In exercises designed to help you prepare for a resolution meeting, we'll touch on hot-button issues such as career change, financial planning, and living up to responsibilities. Hopefully you will be as motivated as we were when you read the true story of one couple's journey from stress to strength, and as inspired by the lessons we share from people who have been through big changes and stayed together.

Why Are We Arguing?

Couples argue for a million different reasons, but at home we often argue because we are overwhelmed by all of the things that we have on our plates. Deep down inside (maybe not even that deep), we are also angry that the other person can't make it all go away. Why can't they just do the laundry, figure out the retirement plan, get the house painted, and find a piano teacher for the kids? This is the consequence of not having clearly defined roles at home. At work you know exactly what you are supposed to be doing—it's right there on your job description—but when you don't take the time to divvy up the to-do list at home, you argue. Who wants to walk in the door and be greeted with the twenty things that "someone" is supposed to take care of? For most of us, especially during a busy workweek, that "someone" (at least in our minds) is our partner.

To make this chapter work for you, the first thing you will need to let go of is the expectation that your partner is going to fix everything. You must also try to let go of the expectation that he should know what needs to get done, that he should meet your timeline, and that he should know your priorities without your communicating about any of it. By following the advice in the early chapters concerning job descriptions, you can avoid the blame game because you will both know exactly who is doing what. Of course conflicts will still come up, but let's hope they won't be based in the unrealistic and unfair assumption that it's your partner's job to make it all go away.

When you do find yourself in a conflict, step back and take a look at what you are bringing to it, because we all need to be responsible for our own moods and stress. If you have had a hard week at work or you are dealing with a highly stressful client, don't bring it home and dump it on your family. Compartmentalizing your emotions a bit benefits everyone in your life at work and at home. Just think how unprofessional it is when someone brings personal drama into the office. Well, it's sort of the same as coming home furious at your boss and then flying off the handle when there are dishes in the sink. It isn't realistic to think that you will be able to keep everything separate, but making an effort to not misdirect your professional frustration toward the small stuff at home will go far in reducing how many squabbles you engage in with your partner.

Arguing More Than Usual

When you find that you are arguing more than usual about the small stuff—scheduling, meal planning, socializing— then maybe it's time to make some changes in how things are getting done. You may need to reduce your expectations for how much you can accomplish every week or you might need to explore getting some help. It could also be time to have some fun. That's right, fun. You remember that? Skipping out of the office a little early to meet each other at a dive bar for a beer? Movies at eleven in the morning with coffee and a bag of popcorn? Taking a long weekend out of town? Okay, so maybe these kinds of "fun" things are harder to do, especially once you have kids, but you can still get a babysitter and go out, or take a family hike, or plan a family road trip. The point is that when the tension starts building, you might need to change direction a bit, step back, and enjoy each other again.

Here are some tips on making time for fun that we learned from the many couples we interviewed for this book (and no, we didn't include the sexier suggestions):

- Have breakfast together after getting the kids to school and before heading to work.
- Get a babysitter for a few hours on a Saturday or Sunday afternoon and go shopping, out to a museum, or to a matinee.
- Pack a lunch and go on a day trip to a nearby park, the beach, or an interesting town.
- Go retro and go bowling.
- Have a potluck dinner party with a few family friends.
- Trade off deciding how Saturdays are spent . . . you never know what you'll end up doing.
- Plan a weekend away, somewhere you've never been before.
- Have a "rediscovering the classics" movie night.

- Research a vacation and then take one.
- Learn something new by taking a class together.

Obviously, these are just suggestions, and what you find fun might be completely different. We really want to encourage you to make the time to enjoy yourselves, especially when things are tense.

How to Manage a Tough Discussion

Don't Try to Have a Rational Discussion When You're Tired

You most likely won't be dealing with a sensitive issue in the office at 11:00 p.m., but at home this could happen every night. Those late-night "discussions" are rarely productive. If you are tired, you can have a hard time hearing the other person and you can often be impatient. Since the key to having a healthy discussion is listening to your partner, agree to table the disagreement until you are both rested.

Tone Down the Drama

When you are in a disagreement over a project at work, chances are good that you don't point a finger at your colleague and say something like, "You never listen to my ideas!" but at home it could happen. Sentences starting with "You never . . ." or "You always . . ." will get you nowhere fast. Try phrasing things in ways that don't place blame, such as, "I feel like my time doesn't matter to you when . . ." or "I get frustrated by . . ."

Don't Fight When You Are Furious

Take a breath, step away, count to fifty, or whatever you need to do in order to rein in your emotions—do it before you start discussing anything. In the office you quickly will be labeled a crazy person if you start yelling at your colleagues out of frustration. That pressure to remain professional and adhere to socially acceptable behaviors actually helps tamp down emotions that could crop up during the workday. Adopt some of this at home and you just might find yourself having a reasonable discussion even when you are angry.

Keep Your Ego Out of It

A healthy discussion isn't about winning, it is about considering the other person's point of view and working together on a solution. You are in this as a team with shared goals, even if you don't happen to agree at the moment. Egos have no place on a workplace team or a home team. Just think about the colleague who won't accept another point of view on a project because she is so wedded to her own. We know what happens to move that project forward: nothing. So keep your ego out of things at home, too.

Be an Engaged Listener

Confirm what your partner is saying or asking for. Asking questions like, "So, you need me to be less critical when you do the homework with the kids?" will let the other person know that you are hearing what he is telling you. Caitlin tried this at work the other day with a colleague who, honestly, she finds incredibly difficult. Rather than push back on what this colleague was telling her, Caitlin just listened and then confirmed what was being told to her. The difficult colleague had a complete turn-around and started to ask Caitlin's opinion on a campaign she was working on. Soon the colleague was doing the listening.

Know That There Are Two Sides

Accept that the other person might have a completely different take on the issue from yours. Don't let this derail the discussion, because it's a simple fact that you are two different people . . . sometimes very different people. The point isn't to change your partner's mind, it's to be heard and work together on a compromise. In the office you are working with essentially strangers. Even if you have known a colleague for years, how well do you really *know* her? This distance between people at work makes it easier for you to accept another take on an issue because you already see her as other than you. At home it's too easy to slip into the "shoulds": My partner "should" see this issue the way I do. My partner "should" see that I'm right. Give it up. People make up your family and people are all different.

Give an Argument Your Time and Whole Attention

There is no place for multitasking when you are trying to work things out with your partner. Put down the iPhone and give your full and undivided attention to the person in front of you. The funny thing about this reminder is that it would probably never occur to you, when in a tense conversation with a colleague, to lean over and check your BlackBerry. Why? Because that would be rude! Yet at home, these boundaries are crossed all the time . . . and not always for the better.

Stay in the Here and Now

It is so easy when you are frustrated or angry to dredge up issues from the past. Don't. You will get off track and open old wounds. Focus on finding a solution to the current issue. Recently, Caitlin found herself in a familiar situation with her difficult colleague. It was yet another important meeting that her colleague "forgot" to invite her to. But did Caitlin pick up the phone and start saying things like, "You always do this" or "Here we are again?" No. Approaching a colleague with an accusatory tone while dredging up the past is just ridiculous. Try *not* doing this at home. The past is the past.

Be Polite

Make sure you both get a chance to express your points of view and even vent your frustrations. Don't push back, because that will only derail and prolong the conversation. Again, at work we are following certain social rules that keep us from stepping across boundaries and bringing emotion where it doesn't belong. Try setting up some of these boundaries at home and both agree to what you find acceptable and unacceptable behavior during a heated discussion.

Look for the Big Picture

When frustrated, remind yourself of the end goals: to fix a communication problem, to find a new way of doing things, and to improve your relationship. Big-picture thinking always helps when you are in the middle of a tough discussion because, in the grand scheme of things, most arguments are a waste of time.

Getting Good at Listening

You know the colleagues at work who interrupt, talking over people in order to hear themselves? How about the ones who pick up their BlackBerry in a meeting to check messages when someone else on the team is talking? And don't we all know the colleagues who will offer up an idea as their own, even though it had been presented by a coworker minutes before? Listening is a skill that is all too rare in the workplace. In fact, if you look at the successful members of the company, we're guessing most of them are good listeners.

Listening to someone shows that you care about what he has to say and that you respect or at least want to consider his opinions, and you like him enough to give him your full attention. When you don't listen and are distracted by your own need to be heard or by e-mails from other people, or don't focus enough to pay attention to what others are sharing, then you are telling everyone that you don't care. Notice how you interact with your colleagues at the office. Are you really listening to what they are telling you throughout the day? Do you turn off your computer during the conversation? Do you let them speak? Or do you interrupt?

So what about at home? Have you been accused by your partner or your children of not listening to them when they are sharing something with you? Do you check e-mails during dinner? Do you interrupt them? We are guessing that if you are like most of us, there is room for you to improve your listening skills. And this is important, because improving listening skills will improve the quality of your relationships, make it easier to work through tough discussions, and make you a better partner and parent.

Listening 101

1. Make eye contact with the speaker when she is talking. Don't look around the room, at your phone or the clock, but, rather, directly at the speaker. Turn off the television or music, and if you need to close the door, then do so.

2. Active listening means paying attention to subtext and the emotions under the words. If the person you're having a conversation with isn't looking at you, is facing away, or is giving you other hostile signs such as crossing his arms, he is most likely angry.

3. Demonstrate your engagement in what is being said by offering up responses like, "I can see that" or "That must have been frustrating" or "You handled that really well."

4. Unlike at work, where you need to think about the appropriate answer while your manager or employee is talking to you, at home you can just sit back and listen to what is being said. You can really be "in" the conversation rather than plotting how to position yourself during the conversation.

5. Show interest in what the other person is saying. Ask follow-up questions that don't bring the conversation back to you.

From the Desk of . . .

Dr. Gary Schuman is a consulting psychologist and president of CDL Consulting, Inc., a human resources consulting and training firm. A frequent speaker on the topics of change, management, coaching, leadership, and career development, Dr. Schuman has advised a wide range of organizations including Apple, MTV Networks, Simon and Schuster, and The Gap.

We asked Dr. Schuman to draw on his consulting experience to offer the steps couples can take to make the most of a meeting to resolve conflict.

Get Ready to Speak Your Mind

According to Dr. Schuman, "The best way to prepare for a meeting of this sort is to spend some time up front creating the key bullet points the individual wants to make during the conversation." To reduce the anxiety the participants might be experiencing before jumping in on a tense topic, "write out both the way you want to frame the conversation and your opening statement." Finally, just as you might for a work presentation, "practice your opening in front of someone else—ideally someone who will be honest with you about what needs improvement—and ask for candid feedback." No need to be this formal at home, but we highly recommend taking a little time to plan for a tough discussion. Have your talking points ready and specific examples to back up the issues you'll raise.

Make the Most of the Moment

Dr. Schuman reminds us that working together to resolve a conflict starts with being "clear in your mind that it's not about winning." There is a common goal *here, which is "to get the issues on the table and find a resolution that works." For people who might be used to speaking without listening, "being able to get into that solution-oriented mind-set is a major shift that most couples have a hard time executing." To create a safe environment for this type of discussion, Dr. Schuman advises setting a ground rule "that if someone is not being heard, he gets to call a time-out." Remind yourself that you are on the same team with the shared goal of working through the issue. Winning won't get you anywhere when it's your partner you have beaten.*

Take the Next Step

To make the most of a conflict resolution discussion, "at the end of the initial conversation you both need to write down whatever was agreed to." Schedule a follow-up conversation so that both of you can check in to see how the agreed-upon actions are being implemented. Dr. Schuman emphasizes that for things to be resolved, "there needs to be a conversation about what has improved or not improved and how well the issue has been addressed." It is always a good idea both at work and at home to leave a meeting knowing what your next steps are. At the end of the discussion, writing down what has been decided between you will keep you focused on the solution that you have reached together rather than the tension leading up to the conversation.

True Story: VP and Mother of Four (*Four!*)

Sharon Kyle leads a crazy life. She is the VP at a busy media company with a team of six direct reports. She commutes into work from four hours away three days a week and works from home the other two. As she juggles the Amtrak schedule and puts out various fires at her company, she parents four kids under the age of nine. Yes, she has a full-time nanny, but her husband works out of the home too, which makes every sick day a minor crisis. We spoke to Sharon, a woman who is very committed to her professional growth, about her two roles—mother and employee—and which skills she can use in both.

Translatable Skills

Sharon tells us that the skills she uses most both at work and at home include patience, managing for long-term growth, and multitasking. "All parents need endless reservoirs of patience to deal with the constant barrage of questions, fighting, events, problems, and tantrums that occur at home. All of these issues happen in the workplace, too." Sharon advises that when you encounter a tantrum at work or at home, take a deep breath and walk away instead of getting pulled into a fight. As for managing for long-term growth both at work and at home, the day-to-day challenges can feel overwhelming. "Try potty training a resistant toddler—it can go on for what seems like forever. The same thing happens at work. I was always amazed that I could leave work for weeks during my maternity leaves and come back to the same problems and the same conversations with no progress at all."

Sharon's advice is to always focus on how things could improve over the next six to twelve months rather than get bogged down in the daily setbacks. She says that she finds it really helpful "to envision what things will be like one year from now and then figure out a way to get there." Finally, multitasking is both Sharon's "greatest strength and curse." At any given moment, she tells us, "My brain is trying to juggle the many things I need to take care of during the day, so I fit in tasks whenever I can." This isn't always a good thing, because sometimes the only way to move forward on something, both at work and at home, is by giving it your full attention.

We think that all of Sharon's professional tips can apply

to helping you run your household. Throughout *Family Inc.* we have encouraged you to start looking ahead to where you want your family to be a year or ten years from now. In chapter 3 we suggested that you take these goals (retirement planning, funding college, family vacations you want to take, home renovations) and break them down into steps, then take those steps and incorporate them into your weekly to-do lists. Before you know it, you will be able to start making inroads into the bigger life goals. We also agree with Sharon's suggestions to tone down the multitasking in order to focus on what really needs your attention. It is so easy these days to become distracted by our iPhones and BlackBerrys, but how good a job are you doing as a partner and parent when you aren't fully present? Caitlin's company has a rule to leave all devices behind when attending meetings; we suggest that you do the same at the family dinner table, homework time, and whenever you are conversing with your family.

Sharon's Life-Changing Class

When Sharon started her MBA program, she was told that the most important class she'd take was Organizational Behavior and, in fact, was told by one friend, "OB is everything." Even though while taking the class she doubted the validity of this statement, afterward, when entrenched in workplace dynamics, she realized that organizational behavior is the key to a successful business. She tells us, "You can have the brightest and best on your team, but if no one is getting along or they are not communicating effectively, then business will suffer." Sharon agrees that the same is true in the family dynamic and that the more people you add to the family, the harder it is to get everyone on the same page. "It is hard to get four kids in good moods and all wanting to play nicely with each other, which is when I use all of my OB workplace skills to actively manage our family dynamic." Just as at work, Sharon is constantly thinking about how she can "team up kids on projects and develop their relationships with each other."

We love the idea of looking at your entire family as a team. As with any group of people, your family comes with complicated dynamics and diverse personalities. But just as at work, you can unify your home team by appreciating the varying points of view, considering the needs of the individuals in the group, and working together to create a vision for the future, followed by laying down the steps to get there.

Unexpected Upside

Before Sharon had children she would write off difficult coworkers, but now she tries to humanize them and figure out what makes them tick. Her experience with the challenging stages any child goes through has made Sharon both more patient and more compassionate to those she works with. "It may sound corny, but I try to remember that everyone has someone who loves them, and that helps me let go of bad workplace behavior."

While the focus of *Family Inc.* has been on bringing home the workplace skills, we could have easily written a book about bringing your parenting skills into the office. You learn so much as a parent, including just how much patience you have in reserve, how to balance the needs of others with your own, and how to give attention to everything and everyone, all the time. All of these skills make you a better manager, if not a better employee.

Management Styles at Home and at Work

Like many of us, Sharon's management style at home is very similar to her management style at work. "I tend to be very hands-off, trust that people will act their age and shoulder their fair share of responsibilities, but I'm willing to step in if they're not." And she tries not to micromanage at work or at home because "no one really likes to be treated like that."

We know that Sharon's willingness to let the people in her life be responsible for their own workload, both at work and at home, cuts down the amount of tension she has with her personal and professional colleagues. The more you micromanage, the more you'll end up doing because you will only meet resistance and resentment from those around you.

Sharon's Most Important Employee

While Sharon tries to be a fair boss both at home and at the office, she "bends over backward" to accommodate her nanny, Mary. Sharon said that without Mary, her "entire ecosystem crumbles," so she "treats her like gold." Sharon gives her raises even in down years, will give her extended vacations to visit her family in Sri Lanka, and gives her as much time off as possible so that she has time to herself. Sharon doesn't count sick days, and she'll loan Mary money if she needs it. "I recognize that while Mary is very good at her job, she is not a workplace professional. So, while I would be appalled if one of my work employees asked to borrow money to take an extended vacation, I am not appalled when Mary asks me if she can do so." One thing that Sharon does practice, both at home and at work, is keeping up her "professional and personal boundaries."

When we first interviewed Sharon on her employees and she identified one that was the "most important," we had a hard time wrapping our heads around treating one person better than the others on the team. But then we thought about office dynamics and it made complete sense. The essential members of any professional team are treated differently. It could be with a title, salary, more vacation time, the window office, or a bonus. At home, it's the same thing to Sharon. Her nanny is the linchpin that keeps everything together. Without her nanny Sharon wouldn't be able to do her job, so obviously she values her above even those employees at the office and therefore has different rules for her. We recommend stepping back and identifying your most important people in your personal life who help keep the trains running on time. Do you show your appreciation? If you pay them, is it enough? Is there anything you can do today to help make things better for them?

Schedule Queen

As in every busy household, Sharon finds that communication is always an issue. "Generally, I manage the family schedule. My husband is good at many things, but he has no interest in the minutiae of keeping track of four little people. It took me a few years, but I've come to accept this." Like others we've interviewed, Sharon has a kitchen calendar where she notes big changes to normal schedules such as business trips, vacation days, Mary's days off, work events, and social commitments. Then each week Sharon writes up a complete weekly schedule for the nanny, part-time babysitter, and her husband that "details exactly where each kid needs to be at any given time and who is responsible for getting that kid to and from that activity.

"In general, I will also e-mail my husband specific dates and times that he needs to help with any out-of-the-ordinary activities." Sharon confesses that the scheduling is one area where she does micromanage, "but if I don't keep track of it, no one else will!"

Sharon has created aspects of her job description without even knowing it by taking on those household tasks that she is naturally good at. Her professional skills, including her ability to organize and schedule, to plan and communicate, are now helping to service the needs of her household. As we discussed earlier in the book, when you combine your skills with the tasks on your family to-do list, everything will run better at home.

Chores Inside the House and Out

As for the household chores, Sharon says, "It's a fairly simple division of labor. I take care of things inside the house and he takes care of things outside the house." For Sharon, that means she handles such tasks as laundry, grocery shopping, meals, and paying the bills. Sharon's husband does the gardening, handles auto repair and maintenance, takes out the trash, and other "outside" duties. Sharon trusts that he keeps up with his chores and he trusts that she keeps up with hers. "If I need extra help with something, then I have learned the hard way to ask for help instead of getting angry that no one is jumping in."

Without officially sitting down and dividing everything up, Sharon and her husband have found a system
that works for them. As we know, without actually taking
a look at who is doing what, the road to finding a fair delin-
eation of labor can be a little bumpy. So while Sharon and
her husband eventually came to a comfortable place with
their to-do lists, they have been married for ten years and
even Sharon said it wasn't easy. We recommend that you
go through the exercises we laid out in the earlier chapters
and have conversations now about what needs to go into
running the home.

A Final Note

Sharon believes that she is a much better professional
than she is a parent. "After all, I have been in the workforce for more than twenty years, and a parent for only
nine. So I have a lot more practice at being a professional."
What we found interesting is that Sharon feels as if she is
constantly facing new challenges as a parent, whereas at
work there isn't anything new: Finance people want ROI
(return on investment), sales people want support, and
bosses want everything. She is already looking forward
to being a grandparent, when she will finally be a "child-
rearing expert."

Tips for Approaching
a Tough Discussion

Your spouse has forgotten to pick up the dry cleaning he said he would get, paid the bills late, and forgot to tell you about a work event that caused last-minute child care drama. You are furious, frustrated, and ready to blow up, or you are doing everything you can to avoid an uncomfortable conversation. *Stop!* Take a breath and gather control over your emotions. Approaching a tough conversation at home is really no different from having one at the office, and here are steps you can take to prepare for either one.

Make an Appointment

If there's an issue on your mind, try not to address it spontaneously or in anger. Instead, flag it when it comes up, or perhaps in your weekly meeting, and make a plan to talk about it. You will be calmer and more rational when you have the discussion if you give it a little time. At the office when you need to have a tough conversation with your boss or an employee, you don't just walk into her office and spring it on her—you make an appointment. Do this at home, too.

Give Yourselves Enough Time

The appointment should take place during a relatively quiet time in the day or week, and the time should be somewhat open-ended. For example, you could plan to talk over breakfast one morning, or in a café or restaurant if necessary, to minimize distractions.

State Your Problem Clearly and Give Examples

When you and your spouse sit down to talk, have your problem thought through and express it as succinctly as you can to make it as easy as possible for your spouse to understand. Have at least three examples at the ready to illustrate what's on your mind.

If You're Doing the Listening, Be Open to the Problem

If your spouse is expressing a problem she has in your relationship, you will most probably feel criticized. Be open to hearing what she is trying to tell you and do your best to hear the truth in it. You don't have to agree, but you need to be able to hear and consider it dispassionately.

Talk It Out

Once the problem has been expressed, there are three ways for the conversation to go. The first is that your spouse agrees with what you have said, thanks you for bringing it up, and agrees to work on it. The second is that your spouse disagrees. The third is that your spouse agrees somewhat but has a different point of view.

Work It Out

The two of you should engage in a conversation about how to solve the problem at hand. This is when compromise is essential. If necessary, or if tempers begin to flare, schedule a follow-up meeting and do some thinking on your own before the next sit-down. Some quiet reflection never hurts.

Leave with Action Steps

At work, tough conversations don't just end; there are usually next steps that one or both of the parties have to take. This is so the employees are actively working toward resolving the conflict. Once you've both had your say, spend time identifying a few next steps that you can each take to make sure this same issue won't crop back up.

Let's Compromise

In the Merriam-Webster dictionary, the definition of compromise is "settlement of differences by arbitration or by consent reached by mutual concessions." Sometimes, when it comes to fights at home, mutual concession is the best approach. The next time you are mid-disagreement, spend your energy looking for a way to compromise and let go of trying to win. Sure, neither of you will get exactly what you want, but you will be able to move through your argument and hopefully end it. It may not be equal, but as long as you are both walking away comfortable about what you are giving up, a compromise will allow you to put the issue to bed. Just as in the office, you will get a lot further at home if you both take the "we're on the same team" approach to the discussion.

We hope that after reading this chapter, you are a little more confident about addressing any issues you may be having with your partner and that you are comforted by the notion of your both being on the same team. Conflicts are inevitable, and they are usually a sign that something has to change. Being willing to do things differently and being willing to accept another point of view are the basis for having a constructive resolution to conflict. Since, hopefully, you are now finding it easier to work through the challenges and make the changes suggested throughout *Family Inc.* with minimal tension and maximum optimism, you are ready for our final chapter.

8

new year, new us

THE ANNUAL MEETING

Once a year, most well-run companies take stock of how things are going. With employees it takes the form of salary and performance reviews. Corporate taxes force chief financial officers to take a look at the profit and loss statements. Insurance rates usually go up every January, making it a good time to pull out existing plans and look for better options. Organizational charts are studied for redundancies and budgets are critiqued. If the lease is up or the company is outgrowing its space, then it's also the time to start looking for a new headquarters. Based on findings, major and minor changes are made and the company starts out a new year more efficient, streamlined, and hopefully in a place to make more profits. This chapter is about bringing that process home in the form of an annual meeting, where you'll take a long, hard look at:

- Everything and everyone you pay to keep your personal life running
- Dreams and goals
- Finances
- Potential or expected changes that could impact your family so that your household can also be more efficient, streamlined, and profitable

This annual meeting is a time to clean house, get organized, evaluate the people who help you run your home, and take even greater strides toward those dreams and goals that you've kept in mind while working through this book. Before you can sit down and make any decision about what and who needs to change over the upcoming year, you'll need to get the lay of the land. To get you started, this chapter includes advice to help you take a close look at everything from your physical space and "service providers" (dentists, child care providers, accountants) to your family insurance plans and overall financial landscape.

Exercises in the early sections of this chapter will help you to look ahead and consider how your circumstances may be changing over the upcoming twelve months (a baby on the way, a child off to college, a mother-in-law coming to live with you) and how they may affect everything from your finances to your living situation. To help you with planning for any financial changes, consider engaging the services of a financial planner, who will offer tips for saving and investing your money. If you decide not to hire a financial planner, then you can find tips and advice online. (We've listed some of the better ones in the "Sources" section at the back of this book.) You will be asked to give some thought to big-picture goals and dreams, the kind that seem unachievable during a busy week, such as buying a new house, starting a small business, or taking a month off. To inspire you, we've included the true story of a couple who supported each other's professional dreams even though it required radically changing their lifestyle and cultivating a lot of faith.

By participating in the exercises, reading the stories, and taking the advice of the experts interviewed throughout this chapter, you'll walk into the next year with an action plan for achieving all of your big and small goals, with a clear head and a well-organized home and family.

The Year Behind Us

The annual meeting is about two things: looking back at the year before and planning for the year ahead. Looking back at the decisions of the last twelve months—your finances, your family culture, goals that were achieved (or not), projects that were completed (or not), improvements to the communications between you and your partner (or not)—can help you create the list for what you want to change and focus on in the upcoming year.

When looking back at the last year, ask yourself if you used any of the tools you learned in this book to help you manage your home better. Did you divide the household responsibilities in a way that is comfortable for both of you? Did you have weekly meetings and were they help-ful? Did you install and use a calendar in the kitchen? Here are a few other areas that you may want to concentrate on when looking back at the last year.

Family Time

Did you spend quality time with your partner and your family? Did you take time to explore and learn something new together? Did you bring your children into the day-to-day running of the house to help them feel a part of what goes on at home?

Finances

Where and how did you spend money last year? On the right things? Are your savings on track? Is your retirement plan a solid one? The time you spend assessing this would be a good time to start gathering your income tax paper-work for your accountant.

Your Support Team

Do you have the right people in place to help you with your taxes, insurance, banking, retirement, and medical needs? Did anything happen in the last year to support or question this? What about your child care situation? Do you have reliable, trustworthy, and accessible child care? Do you need to adjust the nanny's compensation in any way? Is there someone missing from your support team? If so, have you taken steps toward filling that position? If you choose to do certain tasks, such as taxes, on your own, how are you ensuring that you perform them as accurately and efficiently as possible?

Career

How was the last year for you? Any shifts that are negative enough for you to think about making a change? Did the demands of your job impact your home life?

Your Housing

Does your space fit your needs? Any changes over the past twelve months that might require some adjustments at home? When Caitlin left her business a few years ago to work from home as a consultant and a writer, we had to expand the home office to accommodate her computer, files, and books. Did you do all of the updates and repairs that you had planned for over the year, or are there things you should add to the list for this new year?

Vacations

Did you take a family vacation last year? Was it long enough and did you go to the right place? Did it fit into your budget or was it a stretch? If you could not go on vacation this year, why not? Have you taken any steps to ensure that you will go on vacation next year?

As you look back, we are guessing that there are things you would have done differently. We are also guessing that you would have spent less and saved more, that you would have taken more time to be with your partner and your family, and that you would have focused a bit more on moving your career to the next level. Good news . . . it's a *new year*!

The Year Ahead of Us

A new year presents the opportunity for a fresh start. If there are things you should have done differently last year, start adding these as goals (resolutions). A new year is also a great time to look ahead at what changes may impact your home life. When Andrew was hired for a book-writing project that would require international travel, we had to factor that into our yearlong planning because the research trips would impact both our budget and child care options. The year that Caitlin realized that she had to leave the business she co-owned, she and Andrew had to figure out how to make the new budget work over the upcoming months. Discovering we were pregnant with twins obviously sparked months of conversations about budget, scheduling, and hiring some help. Whatever new events may be on your horizon, it is a good idea to at least present them as possibilities.

Following are a few changes to consider when thinking about the upcoming year.

Your Family

If your family is growing, shrinking (a child off to college), or changing (child entering school), that will impact everything about your home life. You might be spending less or more, you could need more or less space, you could need to hire help or fire help if your kids no longer need a babysitter.

Your Job

Take a close look at your position and your company. Are you poised for a promotion? Are there rumblings of future downsizing? Is this the perfect time to start planning for that business you've always wanted to start?

Your Retirement

Are you on track with your retirement planning, or did you fall behind on contributing to your funds? Are there health issues that may impact how much you should be saving? Are you looking to shift your anticipated retirement by a few years and so want to make sure to readjust how much you save?

Your Health

Has a health issue cropped up for you or anyone in your family that is going to change your insurance needs? How much do you want to save to cover out-of-pocket medical expenses?

Education

Will your kids be changing schools and will that impact your budget or schedule? When our kids were ready for kindergarten, we had to move because they were zoned for a school that wasn't great. We spent the year before looking for an impressive public elementary school. After lots of calls and site visits, we ended up moving from Manhattan to Brooklyn. The fact that our kids were entering kindergarten sparked a radical change (new home, new borough, new neighborhood, new friends, new commute) that required lots of planning.

The Economy

The rocky economy of 2008 affected most of us, and not in a good way. As you are looking at all of the changes that could affect you in the upcoming year, you have to consider the economy and the possibility of another crash. Review your investments or speak to your financial adviser about how to protect your savings while still growing your nest egg.

Some changes are unexpected and can't be planned for. But if you think through the possible "what-ifs" and incorporate a buffer into your annual planning, you can help offset, or at least diminish, any drama.

Your First Resolution: Master the List

You may have a bunch of resolutions this year, but you absolutely must make mastering the to-do list your first one. There is an art to making a successful to-do list, a combination of realism and ambition. It can't be too long and therefore unachievable, but it can't be too simplistic either. At the end of the day or the week, you need to be able to cross out items and know that you made some headway. Caitlin was a list-making fanatic at work but wasn't so great at doing it at home. In fact, her lists were a bit of a disaster—full of tasks that couldn't be done in a week or even a month. One year at our annual meeting we decided to get better at our personal lists—to make them tools that could actually help us plan the week ahead rather than becoming futile exercises. To jump on our resolution, we considered Caitlin's work habits. At the office Caitlin's to-do list sits on her desk, updated each night before she leaves for home, ready and waiting for her the following morning. Before a vacation, she will revisit her projects and responsibilities and make a list of what needs to be done upon her return. The to-dos are grouped by projects and due dates, and the bigger tasks broken into steps. She uses her weekly lists to keep not only herself on track but her direct reports too. She even holds on to the lists and files them in case she needs to keep track of the progress on any one project. However you choose to do a list (and we make several suggestions for how to go about it throughout these pages), just make sure you stick to it.

Your Second Resolution: Stay on Budget This Year

If one of your major goals for the upcoming year is to stay on budget, this section should be helpful. Below you will find a compilation of some great tips from the experts and couples we interviewed. We hope that you'll find these ideas both practical and doable, two qualities you want when it comes to ways to save money!

1. Cash is king (and queen). Rather than using a debit or credit card for your out-of-pocket expenses, set an amount in your weekly budget and take the money out in cash. You will be much more conscious of the dollars you are spending or not spending when you see it come out of your wallet.

2. Keep your receipts. When you review what you've spent over the course of a day or a week, you will get a clear picture of ways you can save.

3. Know what you have. Maintaining and updating your checking account will keep you focused on what is going in and out each week.

4. Focus on *not* spending the money and *growing* your savings. When your eye is on increasing your savings account, not depleting your checking account, your urge to spend will go down.

5. Encourage each other to spend less. This could be trading off on making each other lunch, finding deals, or cooking for the week ahead.

6. To make sure you save, consider opening up a five-year CD account, which penalizes you for taking money out early. Eventually you will get to the point of not even considering taking the money out when you are in a crunch because you will forget it's there.

These are all simple and achievable ways to keep your budget on track. Now, come up with some of your own.

Your Third Resolution: Turn That Big Dream into a Goal

A dream is an idea without a plan. A goal is a dream with an action plan. A big part of your annual meeting should be talking about your dreams and then turning them into goals, goals with actual steps that can be broken down and added to your weekly to-dos.

How do you get from a dream to a goal? The first thing to do is to actually visualize the dream in as much detail as you possibly can. This will help you plan out how to achieve it, and maybe even jettison a few dreams that don't make a lot of sense when examined too closely. We had an ongoing fantasy about leaving New York City to live in Great Barrington, Massachusetts—a town we love that is three hours from Manhattan. We spent time really considering the details of the dream, how much it would take to live there, if we could telecommute. We soon realized that Andrew would still need to come into the city for meetings and dinners several days a week, which would leave Caitlin alone with the kids. Upon closer inspection, our dream wasn't so doable, but in thinking about Great Barrington we also looked more closely at how we wanted to live and raise our kids. Sometimes this type of introspection and discussion only happens when you step back and look at your dream objectively.

Now that you've really considered your dream, and if it still fits your reality, your lifestyle, and your family, determine what steps you need to take to make your dream a goal. On a recent business trip, Caitlin was traveling with her colleague Josh. They started talking about making the decision to leave New York City. Since it turned out that Josh and his wife, Lisa, were in the process of moving out of their beloved apartment in Brooklyn to a new house in Princeton, New Jersey, and Caitlin was in the process of writing about making big changes, she began asking him questions. Josh told us that he "loved" everything about their Brooklyn neighborhood and their dream used to be to buy an apartment there, "but the cost of the real estate and the poorly graded local middle school" were making them think twice about their dream. "My wife always wanted to live in a walkable town, with great schools and affordable housing, so after we gave up thinking Brooklyn was the answer, we started figuring out how to turn our dream into our reality."

Josh and Lisa were then both focused on finding the perfect situation for their family, so together they started by making a list of the steps needed to turn the dream into a goal. The list included things like researching towns within commuting distance to New York City, looking at school reports for these towns, looking at housing prices and availability, drafting a budget for buying a house based on the pricing, creating a monthly budget for commuting by town, reaching out to real estate agents in key towns, looking at properties, buying a house, giving notice to the landlord at the current apartment, packing, and moving by July 2011. Suddenly, their dream of finding the perfect town was now a goal with a date attached. It was then easier to break down the more complex action steps into weekly tasks. The "researching towns within commuting distance" list entry became Saturday afternoon road trips for the family to neighborhoods that were recommended to them. The "drafting a budget for buying a house" became a meeting with their accountant.

All dreams can become goals by considering what needs to go into achieving them and setting a time limit for getting them done. Along the way you might realize the dream won't work, but the process will have shown you something new about your needs or your family's needs or pointed you in a different direction.

Our Thoughts on Family Goal Setting

Caitlin works at a company that requires employees to set five major goals for themselves at the start of each year. The goals are a combination of skills they want to acquire, weaknesses or fears they want to conquer, and projects they want to tackle. Goal setting is a way to put your professional growth into a framework, and seeing them written down is both motivating and inspirational for the employees at the company. Even Caitlin, who has spent years working, enjoys the goal-setting exercise both for herself and for her direct reports.

Now, let's go back home. When your family is only focused on getting through the week and spends little to no time on big-picture thinking, improvements, or changes, then you are missing out on an opportunity to drastically improve the quality of your lives. Goal setting at home is really about creating the kind of life that you want. These can be major goals, like buying a house, or smaller goals, like visiting Europe together. Whatever it is that you seek to achieve, setting goals offers your family something to work toward together.

Sample Goals
- Finances (emergency savings, retirement savings)
- Education (savings for college, continuing education classes)
- Housing (plan for a renovation, room change, expansion, move)
- Physical activity (family gym membership, leagues you may want to join, hikes you want to take as a family)
- Travel (day trips you want to plan, vacations)
- Culture (Are there any changes you can make to your family culture? Less bickering and more support?)
- Public service (Is there charity work you can do as a family?)

We encourage you to brainstorm the goals together. Remember that everyone's input is important, so if your daughter wants a goal for the upcoming year of planning a trip to the water park during the summer, then add that to the list. You want the family to support and work toward the goals of each member in the family. Once the goals have been set, then break them into steps and begin to incorporate them into your weekly lists. Make sure that your kids are assigned steps that will help them work toward the goals they added to the list. So if your son wants to spend some family time on Saturday, task him with making a list of the activities you can all do together.

Achievable Goals

When setting goals, it is important that they are achievable. This takes some clarity on your part. The more specific you are in your goals, the easier it will be to break them down into steps. So while "Get healthy" sounds good, "Save money and buy an elliptical machine for the basement" is a little easier to make happen.

Here are additional tips for setting achievable goals:

- Don't let the list get too long. The longer your lists grows, the less likely it becomes that you will achieve everything on it. Keep it reasonable so you can get the boost of confidence that comes from reaching a goal.
- Write the goals down and stick them where you can see them every day. Bathroom mirrors are always good for this!

- After you state a goal, then add a deadline to it. It's motivating to see a time frame for making something happen for yourself and your family.
- Be flexible and accept that you might change your goals along the way. This is about figuring out what you and your family need and want in your lives, and that can change.
- Set measurable goals. If one of your goals is "Bring the kids to visit Nana more often," restate it that so it's "Book a trip to see Nana once every month."
- Once you have achieved a goal, celebrate it! We actually keep a bottle of just-in-case champagne in the fridge for these types of celebrations.

From the Desk of . . .

We spoke to financial adviser Tara Benstead about financial goal-setting and she offered some helpful advice on buying a house and saving for college, as well as general thoughts about paying down debt.

One Size Doesn't Fit All

Tara tells us, "Every savings goal has a different time frame." When it comes to saving for retirement, depending on your age, the money should be put in long-term investments and the "investment vehicles should match that." She advises us that when planning for short-term or long-term purchases, you may need to invest in "savings accounts, money market accounts, and CDs." Unfortunately, she also told us that we are in a "low-interest-rate environment currently, so you may need to shop around at local banks and even online banks for rates."

When Saving for a House

Buying a home is often the biggest purchase you will make in your lifetime, and also the most important, so for something like a home purchase you don't want those funds to be sitting anywhere risky. Tara tells us that in this case, "Forgo the opportunity for a potentially higher return in order to make sure your principal remains safe." She and her husband use an online-only money market account at ING Direct for savings like this. She tells us, "There is no minimum amount, and the money is liquid and accessible within three business days, but not so accessible so that we can use our ATM card to tap into it." It works well for them and has a slightly higher interest rate than their local bank. She suggests that you "think about whether or not you are disciplined enough to keep those savings on hand and readily accessible or if you should look at a six-month or one-year CD."

College Savings

Most experts say that 529 plans are a wonderful tool for college savings. Tara agrees because "the benefits and tax treatment of the plan make this an attractive alternative to a custodial bank account or savings bonds." Tara also often recommends the plan because parents and grandparents maintain control of the funds. What this means is that once your child or grandchild reaches the age of majority (which varies from state to state, but is usually eighteen), they cannot withdraw the funds without your having a say. You control what happens. "If your child or grand-child runs away to Hollywood to be a movie star, you can change the beneficiary of the 529 to another person."

We did some research on 529s and the plans do vary from state to state. Some states have benefits for residents that others do not. Tara directed us to

American Funds because they offer some helpful tools and information online. As with any of these types of decisions, the best bet is to meet with a financial adviser to help you choose the right plan for you and your family.

Thoughts on Financial Planning

When it comes to financial planning, it is extremely important to prioritize your goals. If retirement planning or protecting your family with life insurance is among these goals, Tara tells us to "look at what dollar amount you are able to put toward your goals each month/year and prioritize." And Tara agreed with our personal adviser, who suggested that if you have to make a choice between saving for retirement or saving for college, you can always borrow for college. There are no loans out there for retirement.

Pay Off Debt or Save?

Tara says that paying off debt is important, but she strongly believes that "it is possible to save and pay down debt at the same time." She tells us that when paying off debt, most people focus on paying down the highest-interest-rate debt first, and then working down. Tara agrees with this philosophy, but she also believes that if you have a small debt that could have a lower interest rate, you may want to work on paying that down first, so that you can feel great about crossing one debt off your list.

Tara "highly recommends" saving for retirement, even if you have outstanding debt, especially if your employer offers a payroll deduction plan. We wrote about this earlier in the book, but if your company matches up to a certain percentage, try to defer at least what the company matches. This is free money. Tara says, "If debts are tight, keep the deductions minimal but at least do something." And remember that some debt is good debt to have. Think about it: If mortgage debt means that you own your home, then in most cases (consult with your tax adviser) you can deduct the mortgage interest on your tax return. That's good debt.

Thoughts on Emergency Funds

We hope that you agree that in today's world, emergency funds are especially important. Tara used to recommend that at least six months of expenses be set aside, but now she leans to between six months and a year's worth. To calculate this number, take your monthly expenses for your basic needs: food, clothing,

shelter, transportation, and health care, and multiply
this by six or twelve. Tara advises us that our "emer-
gency reserves should be liquid and readily accessible,
in a savings account, money market, CDs, etc.—
something that you can easily get your hands on within
a few business days should you need them." The key
to building an emergency fund is to put aside a bit here
and a bit there, even if you can't meet the ideal six
months of savings.

Your Fourth Resolution: Hire an Accountant

If you have decided that this is the year to get your finances, your goals, and your planning on track, then one of your first steps should be to hire an accountant. But how do you find one and what do you look for? What can she do for you? We went back to our accountant, Nancy Adams, to find out.

Hiring Right

Nancy believes that there are several things to consider before hiring an accountant. She told us that first we need

to determine if that person has a "basic level of compe-
tence and training." To do this, you should get references,
check out his degrees, and interview him. She also encourages us to ask them questions such as, "How long have you
been in business?" and "Do you have a degree or advanced
training?"—although she doesn't believe that a basic tax
preparer needs to have an advanced degree.

Nancy encourages us to find out whether the accountant works with other clients who have similar "tax issues
or concerns," so there is a comfort level with your type of
financial setup. We hired Nancy in part because she works
with several entrepreneurs and freelancers, so she was
able to give us advice for navigating those tax issues.

Last, before hiring an accountant, Nancy says it's important to interview him. "You want to find out if you are comfortable with him because you are going to be talking with
this person about some very intimate things, including
finances, your hopes and dreams, your goals, and even your
fears." Nancy points out that along with your comfort level
with him, you also need to be able to communicate effectively because it is "pointless if an accountant talks about
tax or financial planning but you can't understand him."

The First Meeting

Nancy recommends starting this first meeting by "sitting
down and discussing basic things about your finances" as a

way to explore your comfort level with an accountant and her experience with your type of client. She also suggests that you bring your tax returns to this meeting. "Show her your returns so she can understand how complex your situation is and what your needs might be." Nancy suggests bringing in a few years of returns with you so the professional "can get a sense of what is normal for you." She also tells us to share any "changes that you expect in your life, both financial and nonfinancial, because often the nonfinancial things have tax implications of which you may be unaware."

True Story: Layoffs, Silver Linings, and Love

About a year ago we were having drinks with our friend James, a highly successful advertising executive. He told us casually that he had been laid off. This is a man who is at the top of his field, who is wooed by the kinds of companies featured in *Ad Age*, and he was laid off! While we were completely thrown on his behalf, he just shrugged and said, "These things happen." As it turned out, he spent only a handful of months looking for work, secured a few consulting projects, spent time with his daughter, and then landed a great gig.

The Silver Lining

James told us that there were some silver linings to the lay-off. "Well, first, I like to sleep, so for the first time in years I could actually sleep until eight-thirty, but the best thing about not having to go to an office every morning was eating breakfast with my daughter almost every day." For James, the opportunity to spend this time with his child was the best benefit, and he was thrilled that they got so close so quickly. When he was laid off, he reached out to his mentor, who advised him to try not to stress and to take advantage of family time. "I remembered that advice and am glad I had the time with her that I did."

Life presents you with opportunities to reexamine your priorities, so take advantage of these moments to step back. In cases like James's, he was given an opportunity to rediscover the joys of being a parent. Luckily, someone he greatly respects advised him to grab these moments and appreciate them.

How a Marriage Weathers Change

Unlike others we spoke to who are experiencing or experienced a layoff, James and his wife, Karen, didn't really change their roles within their household too radically.

"My wife tried very hard to not put me in the position of Mr. Mom. She knew I was treating the job hunt as a full-time job." Beyond the commitment to finding a new work situation, James and Karen had saved a significant amount of money and received a good package, so Karen wasn't suddenly the only breadwinner. It turned out to be a mutually supportive time for James and Karen because as he was looking for work, she was trying to get a promotion, so there was lots of advice, support, and cheerleading going on.

James and Karen offer an interesting way of looking at roles within the household. While many couples would automatically switch roles when one loses a job or comes back home to work, they didn't, because they knew that James was just not cut out to be a stay-at-home dad. He has always been defined by his career and wanted to continue on that path. The key here is to know what you are good at and want out of life and hold on to that, even when your world is turned upside down.

Changing Priorities

As with any big life change, when your career is derailed or redirected in some way, it offers you the opportunity to really question what you want from your life. For James it was more time with his family. "I just accepted a new full-time job and did negotiate a month vacation because I want a spring, fall, and holiday vacation every year with my family."

We strongly recommend that you take whatever you learn during times of change, remember it, and apply it to your future decision making.

Work Skills, Life Skills

We asked James what work skills he drew on when looking for his next job. "Luckily, I'm a good networker and not particularly shy, but it's more than that. I am a firm believer in professional karma." James helps anyone he knows get work, he helps support as many of his freelancing friends as he can, and he takes interest in his current and former teams. "I believe that it will come back to you in spades and it will make people want to work with you."

We are happy to share that we have known James both professionally and personally and have experienced first-hand his generosity toward everyone in his network—his gift for supporting the people around him fosters loyalty among both his friends and his colleagues.

Looking Ahead

We spoke to James about how the layoff changed his short-term and long-term thinking. He shared that in the short term he just wanted to "keep money coming in, keep looking for a job, and not let any of it disrupt the happiness of the family." His long-term view has been changing over the years. "I will be working until I am very old and will need to look at act three or even act four fairly soon. I'm looking at my future in a new light."

We just want you to remember that your goals should reflect where you are in your life. James has begun adapting his career choices and long-term planning around his age and responsibilities.

Advice for Those Facing a Layoff

James says to "follow your heart and your head," so if you are comfortable taking time off, then do it. If you are comfortable working like a maniac to get a new job, then do that. But he adds, "It's important to remain true to yourself at a time when you may be smiling through the pain, pretending to be confident when you are not feeling it, and getting rejected more than getting positive feedback."

Staying true to who you are and what you want will help you and your family get through any rocky times you may encounter.

Ten Steps to Reorganizing Your Finances

We spoke to several professionals about the steps you could take to start reorganizing your finances. Below you'll find a list of our favorites.

1. Make Files: Set up files for your important financial papers including retirement accounts, individual and joint checking accounts, insurance plans (health, life, auto), rental agreements and mortgages, investments, wills, house title, etc.

2. Keep It Clean: Don't hoard papers unnecessarily. Periodically shred and discard items you don't need (see "Paperwork Guidelines: Filing versus Tossing," page 98). This makes it easier to review files and keeps your office or desk neat and clean, making financial dealings less daunting.

3. Learn to Play the Accordion: Don't just toss your receipts into a drawer or shoe box. Buy an accordion file with at least twelve compartments and keep your receipts according to tax-deduction categories. Your accountant can tell you which categories apply to you, but they may include office supplies, phone bills, transportation, child care, medical bills, and so on.

4. Make an Appointment: Check in with your financial adviser annually to review your short-term and long-term goals. If you are faced with any change that could impact your financial life (inheritance, layoff, promotion), see your adviser for guidance at that time.

5. Take an Interest in Interest: Free yourself from credit cards. Keep an American Express card that you pay off every month, and if you need a Visa or Master-Card, use a debit card that draws from your bank account.

6. Save Postage, Time, and Money: Most banks and utility companies have online bill paying. Once established, it is convenient and efficient, and online banking offers the added bonus of balancing your online checking account automatically.

7. Pay Annually: Car insurance, life insurance, college tuition, and home owner's insurance companies offer you the option of paying quarterly, semiannually, or annually. If possible, we encourage you to pay annually. You only have to write one check, and you won't have to think about it again for twelve months.

8. Say No to the ATM: To avoid the daily trip to the ATM, we recommend keeping petty cash in a kitchen drawer. Buy a ledger to record expenses (this helps you figure out where the money goes each month) and replenish your petty cash weekly to maintain a set amount.

9. Find Automatic Investing Programs: If you have decided to jump into the world of investing, look into automatic investment programs that draw a fixed amount from your bank account each month. It is fairly painless, and before you know it, you will have a nest egg.

10. Be Your Own Bookkeeper: Invest in an accounting pro-gram such as QuickBooks to track your personal finances. These programs allow you to print reports, making it easy to review what you have spent each month, week, or day.

A True Story: Michael and Vera Reach Their Goals Together

When we were looking for a couple to interview who could speak to supporting each other's dreams, we didn't have to go any farther than Michael and Vera. When they first met, almost ten years ago, Vera was in advertising, in a grueling but lucrative position that was very different from her dream to work in the arts. Michael, a professional photographer, has spent most of his career experiencing the vicissitudes that go along with a creative life. Two years ago, with Michael's support, Vera decided to leave her job in advertising and return to school. This was no small decision. To make this work, they had to majorly downsize their lives. Although the changes were stressful, their commitment to support each other's life goals didn't waver. Knowing their story and all of the decisions they've had to make over the past year, we knew they would have some advice for all of us about how to navigate challenging times and how to be there for each other.

Time for a Change

When we asked Vera why she walked away from a lucrative career in advertising to jump into the unknown, she answered, "I had no life outside of work because it is a deadline-driven, client-service business, and even after ten years of experience the demands weren't changing." Her work schedule was manageable until she had a husband and a child, but when her last job turned into a "seventy-five-hour-per-week nightmare," she began to re-evaluate.

When your work–life balance is feeling more out of whack than usual, make time to figure out what it is that is throwing things off for you and your family. Do you need more help at home? Are the demands of your job wreaking havoc on your personal life? Are there adjustments that need to be made and priorities that need to be reexamined?

The Lightbulb

Vera remembers the exact moment she knew she had to make a change: "One of my assistants scheduled a team meeting in the office for one a.m." She decided right then that she needed to leave the business for good. She wanted a satisfactory work–life balance and wanted to love her job. She said, "There wasn't a doubt in my mind that I had to make a change."

Pay attention to these lightbulb moments when your life is telling you that something has to change.

Being Realistic

Vera feels pretty strongly that making this type of change couldn't have happened without the support of her husband, Michael. Luckily for her, it didn't take much to convince him that leaving her career was the best decision for everyone. "My family had only seen me on Sundays for years." They knew it wouldn't be easy; talking about sacrifices and making them are two different things. Vera advised us that making big changes can be hard, especially when the economy isn't strong, and she told us, "It's a bummer to move out of your home and downsize your life, even if your reasoning is sound. It was, in many ways, a painful course correction." And they had the occasional doubts, but all they had to do "was sit down to dinner with the family and they knew they'd done the right thing for us."

Whenever you make big changes, either professionally or personally, be realistic about what the transition may look like. There will be doubts, especially when the changes impact your quality of life, but reminding yourselves of the end goal—whatever it may be for you—can help support you.

Planning Is Always a Good Idea

Michael freely admits he doesn't plan at all. Luckily, he has Vera, who spends a lot of time doing it. One thing she has learned is, "If you're not a good planner, you are limiting your choices later on." She points to debt, which can lock you down, as well as a lifestyle that consumes all of your earnings. You have to "plan in order to give yourself options in the future," and because Vera laid the financial ground-work to support a change, she was able to go back to school.

When it comes to planning, we agree with Vera, who said, "The key to doing it right is by really knowing your priorities." Looking ahead a year or even a few months can be overwhelming when you don't have clear priorities. In Vera and Michael's case, they looked ahead and, based on the fact that their priority was family over career, it made things easier to redirect. To plan effectively, look deep inside yourself and be honest about what is important to you and your family, and then make decisions based on those feelings.

Changing the Model

Vera believes that the ability to support and plan for each other's dreams started with breaking down the "model" of their life. "When we made some big changes, what we really lost was a whole imagined future that we didn't even consciously create." Vera's theory is that your life has a certain momentum—an arc—and when you are unconsciously going through your day, week, or year, you complete the next steps in your imagination as though that is what is supposed to be next. When faced with major decisions, Vera and Michael were able to make them fairly fearlessly, believing that they were the architects of their own lives. She tells us, "Helping your partner realize a dream has the potential to bring you both a lot of joy and satisfaction, and to us, it's worth the risk."

Not all of us can make huge changes fearlessly. Truth be told, we are more cautious when it comes to making big choices. Not that we don't make them: Caitlin quit her business and went freelance before going back to corporate and Andrew quit his job and went freelance for good. So don't question your decision to make changes to achieve goals if you feel a little (or a lot) nervous about it.

The Right Decision

We asked Vera if she felt that they made the right decisions over the past year, even after all of the ups and downs that resulted from her leaving the security of her full-time job. "I would have to say we absolutely made the right decision." Vera had always hoped that in her life she'd have enough money for everything she needed and some of the things she wanted. "I know what I need to earn to afford the lifestyle I want, and I can get it with my new career. Salary is just one part of the picture." For Vera, happiness will come from achieving the right balance of three things she values. "I want to be doing a job I love, earning some money, and spending time with my family." In Vera's case, if all she had was an unsatisfying career that kept her away from home, no amount of money could compensate for what she'd lose.

We really appreciate how well Vera and Michael know each other, support each other, and share the willingness to see their life together as constantly evolving. We also respect how dedicated Vera is to planning, because it gives them a realistic way to make the big changes they need in order to create the life they want.

So here we are at the end of chapter 8. We hope that you feel energized as you sit here looking at any notes you may have taken during your annual meeting and as you reflect on the conclusions you have come to and the changes that you want to make over the upcoming months. Inspiring you to want to take control of your household was the goal we set for ourselves when writing this final chapter. We want you to feel excited about all of the free time you will now have during the upcoming year thanks to hiring the right accountant, using a financial planner, setting some short-term and long-term goals, and having the support of your partner.

final thoughts

An interesting thing happened to us as we were writing and interviewing for *Family Inc.* We realized that we needed this book and all of the advice in here as much as you do. We are, in fact, *you*: a busy, working couple with limited time and resources who juggle nurturing our children, careers, and each other every day. Our life, as our parents often tell us, is "crazy." Yes, before writing the book we had weekly meetings, we were (and are) highly organized and efficient about most things, and we do keep pretty detailed to-do lists. But, as much as we thought we had it all together, we were missing the fun part. We were so focused on maintaining our gift closet, refining our filing system, and keeping up to date on our budget that we weren't using the time we saved—once systems were set up—to enjoy one another as a family.

We somehow forgot the entire point of bringing our

office skills home, that is, to reduce the stress, streamline the work, and evenly distribute the chores with the end goal of having more time for each other. So our lightbulb moment came not when the financial planner told us to sign up for our company's 401(k) plan, because that we had done, but instead when a couple told us that they savor the five minutes they have alone to talk when on a family hike. Soon after that, we had another epiphany when Lori, the social worker we spoke to, suggested that we play word games with the kids rather than jumping right into homework as a time the family can decompress together. And, later still, when a couple told us that they loved to sit and talk about all of the fun places they could retire to. Right! That was the entire point of our creating these systems for ourselves, the point of carving out the free time, and the point of jumping in on financial planning: to *enjoy* our lives together. To have fun, to fantasize, to plan, to learn new things and explore new places, to support each other as we try to achieve our personal dreams and goals. Wow. This was one big lightbulb moment for us, because it put everything back into perspective. It also made doing all of the delegating, communicating, managing, organizing, and planning at home fun again, because we were doing it for a higher purpose, for the good and the happiness of all four of us.

We don't know what you hoped to achieve when

picking up *Family Inc.,* but we really hope that on your list was something about finding the time for each other and for your family. Because the rest of it—becoming an amazing delegator, a better manager, or a clearer communicator and setting up an efficient home office—will mean nothing if you aren't also working to create a more harmonious home.

Our other, smaller epiphany while writing this book occurred when we started interviewing our experts. We realized that our lives now are almost entirely integrated. We no longer put in the Monday–Friday workweeks with the day ending at 5:00 p.m. Our professional and personal lives are merging more and more each year. You can say that you try to keep them separate, but just pull up your Facebook page and look at your friends. We're guessing you will see a few colleagues up there mixed in with your high school boyfriend or girlfriend. Our workdays are creeping into evenings and over weekends, and our iPhones often receive both our work and personal e-mails. And we aren't saying this is a bad thing: Many of us are able to telecommute because of it. With integrated lives come translatable skills, and *that* was our epiphany, that all of those work skills we explored throughout *Family Inc.*—managing, scheduling, organizing, planning—are actually life skills. The systems we use, the conversations we have, the roles we play, the responsibilities we take on are just as relevant at 9:00 a.m. on a Monday as 10:00 a.m. on a Saturday.

So what we are asking our readers to do in this book will help you improve your entire life, not just the hours you are at home. Getting great at delegating is going to help you get the best contribution from your assistant and your mother-in-law. Preparing for financial setbacks at home will inspire you to take another look at your department's budget. Assessing the strength of your team both at work and at home will make sure you surround yourself with people who actually support you. Heightening your awareness for what needs to get done around the house and around the office will make you a better partner and a better colleague, as will learning to be a good listener.

So trust us when we tell you that the time you have spent working through this book is time well spent. The skills you have honed, the weaknesses you have identified, the challenges you have faced will improve the quality of your life . . . period.

sources

Apps to Download

Life Balance (www.llamagraphics.com)
Remember the Milk (www.rememberthemilk.com)
2Do (www.2doapp.com)
Toodledo (www.toodledo.com)
Evernote (www.evernote.com)
Pocket Informant (www. pocketinformant.com)

Books to Read

Time Management

Getting Things Done by David Allen
How to Get Control of Your Time and Your Life by Alan Lakein
The 7 Habits of Highly Effective People by Stephen R. Covey

Relationships

The Seven Principles for Making Marriage Work by John Gottman and
    Nan Silver

The New Rules of Marriage by Terrence Real
Relationship Rescue by Phillip C. McGraw

Websites to Check Out

General Helpful Information

www.ehow.com

Organizing

www.realsimple.com
www.lifeorganizers.com
www.getbuttonedup.com

Time Management

www.tamingtime.com
www.asianefficiency.com

Management

www.entrepreneur.com

Family Wrangling

www.mommytracked.com

Hiring Tips

www.stengelsolutions.com

Financial Advice

Saving for College: 529 Information

www.americanfunds.com

Retirement Planning

www.aarp.org
www.choosetosave.org

Finding a Financial Planner

www.cfp.net

acknowledgments

It wasn't easy to find the time to write a book together, and we'd like to thank the key people who helped us out of the starting blocks and all the way to the finish line, namely, our agent, David Black, who always encourages us to be ourselves on the page and off, and our editor, Sara Carder, who immediately recognized the need for this book and has supported us from the very beginning.

Thanks also to all of the couples and experts who shared their stories, advice, and tips with us.

Lastly, Caitlin wants to thank Andrew for being such an amazing husband and father; Andrew wants to thank Caitlin for making this personal and professional journey so fun and fulfilling.

index

about the authors

Caitlin Friedman is best known for her Girl's Guide series (coauthored with Kimberly Yorio), which includes the bestselling titles *The Girl's Guide to Starting Your Own Business* and *The Girl's Guide to Being the Boss (Without Being a Bitch)*. She has appeared on the *Today* show numerous times and has been featured in *Time*, *Real Simple*, and many other national publications.

Andrew Friedman is the author of *Knives at Dawn: America's Quest for Culinary Glory at the Bocuse d'Or, the World's Most Prestigious Cooking Competition*, and has collaborated on more than twenty books and cookbooks with many of the best chefs in America. As a sportswriter, he is an editor-at-large for *Tennis* magazine and coauthor of American tennis star James Blake's *New York Times*–bestselling memoir *Breaking Back*. He is also the founder of and chief contributor to the website Toqueland.com.

if you enjoyed this book,
we also recommend...

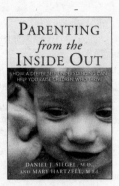